THE PSYCHOLOGICAL BASIS OF MORALITY

LIBRARY OF PHILOSOPHY AND RELIGION

General Editor: John Hick, H. G. Wood Professor of
Theology,
University of Birmingham

This new series of books will explore contemporary religious understand-
ings of man and the universe. The books will be contributions to various
aspects of the continuing dialogues between religion and philosophy,
between scepticism and faith, and between the different religions and
ideologies. The authors will represent a correspondingly wide range of
viewpoints. Some of the books in the series will be written for the general
educated public and others for a more specialised philosophical or
theological readership.

Already published

William H. Austin	THE RELEVANCE OF NATURAL SCIENCE TO THEOLOGY
Paul Badham	CHRISTIAN BELIEFS ABOUT LIFE AFTER DEATH
Ramchandra Gandhi	THE AVAILABILITY OF RELIGIOUS IDEAS
Hugo A. Meynell	AN INTRODUCTION TO THE PHILOSOPHY OF BERNARD LONERGAN
Dennis Nineham	THE USE AND ABUSE OF THE BIBLE
Bernard M. G. Reardon	HEGEL'S PHILOSOPHY OF RELIGION
John J. Shepherd	EXPERIENCE, INFERENCE AND GOD
Robert Young	FREEDOM, RESPONSIBILITY AND GOD
Patrick Sherry	RELIGION, TRUTH AND LANGUAGE-GAMES
Hywel D. Lewis	PERSONS AND LIFE AFTER DEATH
J. C. A. Gaskin	HUME'S PHILOSOPHY OF RELIGION
F. C. T. Moore	THE PSYCHOLOGICAL BASIS OF MORALITY

Further titles in preparation

THE PSYCHOLOGICAL BASIS OF MORALITY

An essay on value and desire

by

F. C. T. MOORE

BARNES & NOBLE BOOKS

BOOKS
10 East 53d St., New York 10022
(a division of Harper & Row Publishers, Inc.)

First published 1978 by
THE MACMILLAN PRESS LTD

Published in the U.S.A. 1978 by
HARPER & ROW PUBLISHERS, INC.
BARNES & NOBLE IMPORT DIVISION

Printed in Hong Kong

Library of Congress Cataloging in Publication Data

Moore, Francis Charles Timothy.
  The psychological basis of morality.
  (Library of philosophy and religion)
  Bibliography: p.
  Includes index.
  1. Ethics.   2. Values.   I. Title.
BJ1012.M627   121'.8   77–22632
ISBN 0 06 494933 8

'If the will did not exist, neither would there be that centre of the world, which we call the I, and which is the bearer of ethics.'

LUDWIG WITTGENSTEIN
Notebooks 1914–1916
p. 80

Contents

(i) *Argument in one dimension*

Books begin at the beginning and continue until the end (footnotes being the exception that proves this rule). This unfortunate one-dimensionality has led philosophers into various expedients of style, from Platonic dialogue to Cartesian autobiography, Spinozistic tabulation or Nietzschean declamation, expedients by which the complex internal relations of argument may be reduced to a tractable linearity.

This book has strayed from accepted linearities. It has a main argument presented in linear fashion. But there are in addition annexed sections which are intended to support parts of that argument, to lead into it, to explain it further, to defend it against various objections, and to show its bearing upon issues related to those arising in the main argument.

The main argument is printed in roman type with section numbers in arabic numerals, while the annexes are printed in italic type, and are separately numbered in roman style. The main argument has a degree of self-sufficiency, while the nature and intent of certain annexes imposed an allusive and sometimes fragmentary treatment.

(ii) The Metaphysic of Morals

In his book Individuals, *Strawson made a distinction between 'descriptive metaphysics', which is 'content to describe the actual structure of our thought about the world', and 'revisionary metaphysics', which is 'concerned to produce a better structure'.*

But is 'descriptive metaphysics', so defined, a task of philosophy at all? It may seem that this is an area of study belonging properly to various of the human sciences. To examine how men actually think, we may say, is in different ways the business of historians, sociologists, social anthropologists, psychologists, and so forth. Such studies have an empirical, rather than a philosophical, orientation.

What is true in this objection accounts, I believe, for some of the traditional hostilities and suspicions that arise between philosophers and others. But it is nevertheless a misleading objection. For philosophy too starts from, even if it does not always return to, how men actually think. Moreover, those very thinkers who might covet the title of 'descriptive metaphysician' customarily argue the existence of ordered relations between concepts, such that some are said to be logically more basic than others, or even such that some are claimed to be a necessary requirement for any thought or experience of any kind. We may put it by saying that such a philosopher wishes to disclose a necessary order within the natural order of thought.

Of course, this characterisation of a philosopher's task by appeal to a distinction between a necessary conceptual order and an empirical natural order raises major problems. We shall return to them in annex (xi) below.

For our present purpose, it is sufficient to observe that in philosophy and elsewhere the search for a 'necessary order' often manifests itself in an explanatory technique by which one set of propositions, concepts or terms is taken as fundamental, and some other set is explained in terms of the first. This is the procedure often given the label of 'reductionism'. Reflection on it will lead us to qualify the distinction between descriptive and revisionary metaphysics.

For the application of this procedure by the so-called 'descriptive metaphysician' to diplay what he claims to be the actual structure of our thought about the world will be the diagnosis of some necessary order within

2

the natural order of thought, and will always be open to challenge. In the case of such challenge, the philosopher who thought he was describing may well be charged with an unnecessary and implausible revision. Berkeley notoriously claims to be a champion of common sense, that is, to be describing the actual structure of our thought about the world. But what of Berkeley's critics? Are they to maintain that he has described wrongly, or that he has revised unacceptably? Or should we reject this dilemma, and claim that Berkeley is neither describing the natural order of thought, nor offering an alternative to it, but proposing a debatable account of a necessary order within the present and perhaps within any possible natural order?

Techniques of reduction, I suggest, whether in philosophy or elsewhere, cannot be justified on the basis of the natural order alone—by reference to brute facts. It is this that has led some to hold that not only are particular applications of such techniques open to criticism, but that they are of their nature vicious. 'Everything is what it is, and not another thing.' Such views constitute a radical and pervasive scepticism. How can dynamics, for example, be justified in treating idealised and not real trajectories? And what remains of the very profession of philosophy? This scepticism is not to be lightly dismissed; but if philosophy can be vindicated at all, it will be improper to object to a particular philosophical argument on the sole grounds that it employs a technique of reduction. In moral philosophy, for example, arguments against naturalism are generally question-begging in their bald assumption of the autonomy of moral concepts. There is no 'naturalistic fallacy' unless it be the fallacy of all philosophy.

I make no excuse, therefore, for arguing what is undoubtedly describable as a naturalistic position in moral philosophy, for offering a metaphysic of morals which is, I believe, truer than Kant's own position to his injunction that 'a metaphysic of morals has to investigate the Idea and principles of a possible pure Will'.

But it is the proper courtesy of an author to apologise to his reader for the imperfections which will certainly be found in his work, and to make it clear that those whom he wishes to thank are named for that purpose alone, and not with the impertinent intention of lending their authority, however subtly, to the finished book.

I am grateful to many colleagues, friends and students from Oxford, Paris, Birmingham and Khartoum, but particular thanks are due to Elizabeth Anscombe, Christopher Bryant, Jacques Derrida, Alec Fisher, Peter Geach, John Hick and Christopher Villars; to Bernard Mayo, Ingmar Pörn and Charles Whiteley, whose comments on the draft were invaluable; to Peter Lienhardt, whose pungent remarks on the dangers of the profession *of philosophy made a lasting impression on me; to the British Academy, the French Government, and the University of Birmingham, for important material assistance at various stages of my work on this book; to M. and Mme. Busnel, in whose congenial house the final draft was written; to Hilary Fancote, for her patient and efficient typing of the draft; to my wife, whose help and indulgence made this work possible; and to Alf Louvre, who said 'It's anarchy!'*

1 The Pure Will

Kant held that it was the will conforming itself to duty, not the will alone, which was to account for morality. I shall argue that the existence of the will by itself already implies the existence of value.

As a first step, we shall make abstraction of the specific human circumstances and contingencies of wills and values as we know them, and address ourselves to the relation between pure will and pure value.

The idea of a 'pure will' is, at its schematic minimum, the same as the idea of a source of change. Consider a universe containing just one such source of change. May changes take place in such a universe other than those produced by this source of change? Any such changes, clearly, would have to be such as not to originate from a source of change; for if they did, our universe would then contain more than one source of change, which is contrary to the hypothesis. Any such additional changes would therefore have to be of one of two kinds: they would be either changes produced by other changes which in turn were produced by other changes and so on (there being no first member in such a series, there would *a fortiori* be no source for any of the changes in it); or they would be changes occurring spontaneously (or produced by spontaneously occurring changes). These two cases—that of causal sequences of changes without a first member, and that of self-originating or unoriginated changes—may be problematic. Indeed we shall find it necessary to consider them further in section 13 below. But they are not obviously incoherent. And, what is important for the present purpose, nothing in the schematic initial condition of our hypothetical universe (that it contain only one source of change) permits us to *exclude* the possibility of changes occurring in it which are not attributable to that will.

We may now assert of this universe that any change that occurs in it must occur by the operation of the one source of change, or spontaneously, or as a member of a sequence of changes each producing the next. These latter kinds of change may not occur, but we cannot exclude them. But if they do occur, a further possibility is introduced—of changes occurring as a result of some combination of the three factors. This possibility must be open, since if it were not there would be no grounds for claiming that the three classes of events belong to the same universe. Moreover, a change which is due to more than one factor may be different from what it would have been if only one factor had been in operation.

We are now faced with a surprising result. It might have seemed that the idea of the pure will, abstraction made of the contingent forms of our actual experience of willing, was the idea of a source of change which would produce any change upon which it was directed without impediment, so that it would be absurd to suppose willing to occur without its corresponding change. But the construction of a model universe even with only one will has led us to require the *possibility* of the frustration of that will. For the model does not allow us to exclude changes attributable to other factors. If there are other factors, we cannot exclude their interaction. And if they interact with the will, we cannot exclude the occurrence of a change other than that towards which the will was directed.

Of course, just as the 'will' in this model universe is no more than the abstract form of agents as we know them, so too the 'value' distinctions which can now be seen emerging are no more than the abstract form of the real evaluations which we make and encounter in our lives. But these forms at least have emerged in our model universe, which is good so far as it conforms itself to the will, and bad so far as it does not, from the standpoint of the one will (*and there is no other standpoint*).

We take issue, then, with Kant's treatment of the *a priori* conditions of morality. An examination of the 'idea of a possible pure will' alone enables us to see in it the genesis of values, though the sketch here offered of a model universe calls for considerable elaboration (such as is adumbrated in annex (viii) and sections 8 and 13 below).

This condensed and abstract argument is a rehearsal for what follows. Our embodied existence, our varying and conflicting desires and pleasures, the intransigencies of the world, of others and of ourselves, all of these greatly complicate the various evaluative and psychological notions which are cast in the moulds respectively of what I have been calling the idea of pure value and the idea of pure will.

It will now be our task to relax the abstractions made, and to move back from the model universe just described to the very world of our joys and sufferings.

(iii) Objects of Desire

But as we turn to give an account of human desires, as a first concrete mode of the 'pure will', we encounter a philosophical reef. For we shall have to consider the objects of desires, and in so doing we shall naturally if not unavoidably speak of states of affairs, and of the propositions specifying them. These are problematic and controversial notions. I do not hope, in this annex, to offer a detailed solution to these problems, but to provide a chart by which my later use of the notions of states of affairs and propositions may be accepted without shipwreck.

We may start by observing the circumstances of our natural and perhaps unavoidable use of these notions. Men respond to states of affairs. They believe them to exist. They believe that they can be brought into existence. States of affairs provoke fear and pleasure. They are perceived and reported by the use of the appropriate propositions. They are striven for. But what account is to be given of these notions?

States of affairs may be envisaged either from the point of view of Wittgenstein's Tractatus *or from the point of view of Carnap. The two extremes (even if these labels for them are not entirely appropriate) are that in which we start from the universe as a whole, and consider a state of affairs as what corresponds to a complete state description of the universe, and that in which we start from the objects which exist in the universe, and consider a state of affairs as a specific combination of some of those objects. In the one, it is the universe as a whole which is supposed in some sense to be given; in the other, it is particular objects which are supposed to be given.*

But in fact neither of these is given. It is not an epistemological difficulty that I am raising here: not the difficulty of how we can know that a given state description of the universe is true, or of how we can know that we have securely identified a particular object, though both of these are difficulties. The problem is more radical. For if the universe is unbounded, then state descriptions of it of the kind envisaged cannot be given, and any partial description will fail in its logically primary task of providing an adequate criterion of identity for states of affairs. Equally, there could be no formally adequate identifying description of a particular object, enabling it to be

7

distinguished from other objects and then to form states of affairs by its combination with some of them. Thus the viability of the notion of states of affairs would depend on whether as a matter of fact the universe is finite.

The readiest solution to those difficulties is to weaken our identity requirements for states of affairs, incorporating into our account provision for the incompleteness of propositions specifying states of affairs, either in the sense of not being complete state descriptions of the universe, or in the sense of not deploying complete identifying descriptions (after the manner of Russell) of the objects composing the state of affairs: the two difficulties in certain respects coincide.

According to this solution we regard a state of affairs as an entity determined only in respect of those features included in the proposition specifying it. It remains undetermined of all other features whether the state of affairs has or lacks them.

An entity of this sort is pretty much a logical weakling: for instance, the law of excluded middle will be severely restricted in its case. Yet it is, I suggest, because of the tractability of a notion of states of affairs allowing this weak identity that human beings can readily deal with and appreciate the situations which they believe themselves to encounter. The provisionality and indeterminacy which is the logical weakness of the notion is at the same time its practical strength. At times, indeed, by variously motivated and effected restriction of our area of enquiry, we behave as though states of affairs were at least in principle fully determinable (in both the two senses formerly indicated), and for the purpose at hand this procedure may be legitimate. But it is a realist extrapolation from (or a creation of simplified model domains within) the prior—and not just epistemologically prior—case of states of affairs which are only partially determined; we should not be misled by it into attributing greater theoretical substance to the notion of states of affairs than it actually possesses.

For the notion is not only logically but also ontologically weak, since we have now made states of affairs relative to propositions held to specify them. The question now arises: what of propositions themselves?

It is a commonplace that here too we find ourselves in face of a form of the old realist/nominalist controversy. According to the realist position, a proposition is the thought of a sentence (at least in the case of declarative sentences)—a thought which a given sentence may succeed to a greater or less extent in conveying, and which may equally be expressed in other sentences, a thought whose existence is not dependent on the existence of any particular linguistic forms, nor on the existence of any particular thinker—a thought which is real—which is an abstract, non-spatiotemporal, non-linguistic, and *non-psychological entity. According to the nominalist position, a proposition—if we are to use the term at all—is a linguistic entity. The view is more or less flexible according to whether and how the phenomenon of 'saying in one's heart' is admitted (thereby providing suitably linguistic entities where they might not else have seemed to be found), and according to the ways in which syntactic or even semantic considerations are made to enter into the criteria for identification of sentences—of the linguistic entities which are the nominalists' candidates for propositionhood.*

On the simplest realist view the same proposition is expressed by the following two sentences: 'The morning star is bright', and 'The evening star is bright'. On this view, true sentences refer to or are made true by their correspondence with states of affairs. And in the present case, the two sentences say the same thing of the same object: they are both true in virtue of the same state of affairs. Consequently the thought they express is also the same. But on this view, as it stands, there is no uniform way of dealing with the non-equivalence of the two sentences in what are called 'intentional contexts'.

We may therefore adopt a modified and more subtle realist view—that of Frege. According to this view also, the two sentences have the same reference, which is not a state of affairs, but a truth value, in this case, truth. However, they do not have the same sense, since the sense of the expression 'the morning star' is different from the sense of the expression 'the evening star', though their reference happens to be the same. Thus though we admit realist propositions, as the sense or thought of sentences, we find them to be different in the case of these two sentences. Hence it is possible to deal with the difficult features of intentional contexts by maintaining that when a sentence appears in such contexts it then has as its reference what in non-intentional contexts would be its sense.

This modified realism provides a coherent solution to the problem at hand. Yet it has an ad hoc character, and introduces an intensional anomaly into the logic of intentional contexts which is plainly going to be awkward to cope with. Our problems are housed, but in a logical ghetto. If we turn to the nominalist solution, on the other hand, we find that the ghetto has been replaced by an unusually characterless suburb. For the essence of this solution is to claim that in these contexts what we are dealing with is not any kind of entity which transcends thought and language, but a particular linguistic form. The immediate reply to such solutions is to state baldly that when, for instance, we attribute a belief to someone, we do mean more than to attribute to him some actual, tacit or potential utterance of some form of words. Moreover, it is clear in the case of human behaviour (let alone the case of animals) that it is false to claim that whenever a man has a desire, a hope, a belief, there exists some form of words which in one way or another he must be taken to be manipulating, even in his heart. For belief in a proposition need not actually take a specific linguistic form at all.

The difficulty we are now presented with closely resembles that which we encountered in the case of states of affairs, and the solution I shall propose is also analogous to that solution. Propositions are characteristically, though not exclusively, expressed by sentences, and when we take a sentence to express a certain proposition, we are assuming in that context the agreement of a certain community, however wide or restricted, about what other sentences would rightly be taken to express the same proposition. It may seem that there is a fatal circularity in such an account of propositions—being of the form: a proposition is what is expressed by any set of sentences which are taken to express the same proposition! However, the agreement of the community is not happily described as an agreement that such and such sentences express the same proposition: it is rather that for some purpose and in respect of some state of affairs, a certain open set of sentences is such that any of them may be substituted for any other without such a substitution making any difference (for that purpose and in that context). Consider, for example, the case where I repeat what I have said in other words to avoid misunderstanding. It is true that when I do this, there is a way in which I am precisely not treating the two sentences as interchangeable. Indeed, I am envisaging the possibility that the first may not perform its desired function, whereas the second (or the first together with the second) may do so. Yet this is possible just because both are equally such as to perform that function (if successful—and of course it would be absurd to search for a guarantee that the hearer understands). Now, the consensus which expresses itself in such functional equivalence (whatever detailed account should be given of it) does not in general enable us to give a complete enumeration of the set of sentences so determined as expressing the same proposition; nor indeed is our assumption of consensus in particular cases always correct.

However, it is a matter of everyday experience that sets of sentences are granted as equivalent. Where this is so, it is appropriate to speak of propositions of such and such a form, since there is then no particular sentence with which we are concerned. Of course, no label of the form 'the proposition expressed by s' can of itself and independently of context identify a particular proposition: as is so for definite descriptions in general. Even where a list of sentences is given, it cannot be a complete list, and will not guarantee community of understanding, which is in general already in existence in the shared patterns of life and thought that are the informal basis for the philosopher's use of the notion of a proposition.

But the case of intentional contexts is precisely one where the community *of understanding may be in question. For the subject matter of intentional statements is the beliefs, desires and attitudes of particular people, something of which for good reasons abstraction is made in other contexts of discourse. Yet this need not lead us to the extreme of claiming that in these contexts there can be no criteria for interchangeability of sentences, as the severe nominalist solution requires, at least in the admittedly unsophisticated version of it which I have indicated. Nor are we obliged to devise a special semantics such as that of Frege. For Frege's account takes as given what I argue to be in question in such contexts, namely the senses of those expressions which will now refer to their senses.*

The fact is that in such contexts, sentences are taken as interchangeable with certain others, and thus as 'expressing a certain proposition'; but whereas elsewhere there is an assumed agreement about the range of sentences in question, the arbiter being communal practice, in these cases, on the other hand, it is precisely in question what proposition the person is entertaining, and it is he alone who is, exceptionally, the arbiter of what other sentences are taken as expressing the same proposition, no matter how unorthodox his understanding.

Of course, when I speak here of the individual being the arbiter, I do not mean that we are to refer the matter to him for adjudication. It is rather that the criteria of what is meant and understood lie now not in communal behaviour, but in his individual behaviour—the way in which his fashion of acting, speaking and thinking shows him to understand the sentence: of this he is not necessarily himself the best, and certainly not the only judge.

The account of intentional contexts that is now taking shape hinges on the claim that their peculiarities are not in fact logical: rather the problems concern the criteria for propositional identity appropriate in such cases, since the identity of propositions in intentional contexts, as has been argued, depends upon the person whose propositional attitude is in question. However, this account seems to encounter a serious difficulty in modal contexts, where the same difficulties (of referential opacity and so forth) arise as in the other intentional contexts already considered, but where there seems to be no possibility of generalising the solution proposed, since we cannot relativise the identity of propositions in modal contexts to some individual person. Thus it may be objected that the account proposed here is ad hoc, being able to cope with a certain problem in psychological contexts, but not with what is in the end the same problem in modal contexts.

However, the approach suggested can be extended to cover modal contexts. Consider the interpretation of the modalities by the semantics of possible worlds. In this semantics, we read, for instance, 'Necessarily $F(a)$' as '$F(a)$ in all possible worlds'. It will be in this way that we shall account for the *failure of the inference 'Necessarily* **F(a)**, **a** = **b**, *therefore necessarily* **F(b)**'. *But what does the adoption of such a semantics amount to? It amounts, I suggest, to the introduction of an uncertainty into the identification of the propositions with which we are dealing—not this time as a consequence of individual vagaries on this side of some agreed identification, but now of vagaries of possible worlds and contexts beyond the agreed identification. If* **a** *may recur in many possible worlds, and so* **b** *also, the identity of the proposition '* **a** = **b**' *is now in doubt. To which world is it to be relativised? (For trans-world identity of objects cannot be assumed, though it may be variously specified, connecting different worlds by structures of what have been dubbed 'trans-world heir-lines'.) If we relativise it to 'this' (agreed) world, then the inference will not stand. But if, for instance, it were true of any arbitrary world, then '* **a** = **b**' *so interpreted becomes equivalent to 'Necessarily* **a** = **b**', *and the inference will stand.*

These are the lines of argument showing that in intentional contexts in general, and not only those where psychological notions are involved, the puzzles that have been so much discussed may be regarded as puzzles about the identity of propositions, and not about logical peculiarities of propositions of a certain type.

I am arguing that we should retain the notion of propositions for intentional and non-intentional contexts, and that there are no logical differences between such propositions arising specifically from the context difference, once the identity of the propositions concerned has been carefully ascertained. Now this position suggests that arguments like ' **a** *believes* **p**; **p** *implies* **q**; *therefore,* **a** *believes* **q**', *are after all valid, and that any appearance to the contrary is produced by introducing confusion about what proposition it is that recurs in the argument. For instance, it is rightly held that 'The morning star is a planet' implies 'The evening star is a planet' granted the truth of 'The morning star is the evening star'. But when it is further assumed that the man of whom we say (doing the best we can) that he believes that the morning star is a planet is necessarily entertaining the same proposition as was expressed in the above argument, then there is dangerous ground underfoot. Indeed, if this man does not believe that the evening star is a planet, this precisely raises questions about what proposition it is that he is being said to believe, when he is said to believe that the morning star is a planet. His ignorance of the fact that the morning star is the evening star must be taken to affect the meaning he attaches to sentences involving reference to the morning star, and sentences involving reference to the evening star. Referential opacity is not a property of a sentence or a proposition: it is in the eyes of the beholder.*

Let us be clear about what is suggested here. In many ordinary circumstances we assume with perfect felicity that we do for the purpose at hand understand each other perfectly. Information is commonly and often justifiably treated as a communal and communicable possession, and investigations are treated as methods of ascertaining the truth or falsehood of propositions quite transparent to the investigators. It is in this common world of the understanding that we act as though we had to do with Platonic propositions.

But as soon as the possibility of misunderstanding arises (and the very existence of a common world of the understanding depends upon there being some means of coping with this), propositions—or their corresponding sets of sentences—become circumscribed. We have to rein ourselves in to that weaker form of identity of propositions according to which they are determined only in respect of a certain limited range of sentences taken as interchangeable. If **a** *does not believe* **q**, *though* **p** *implies* **q**, *then* **a** *does not believe* **p**, *even though he is rightly said to believe that* **s**, *and* **s** *is normally understood to express* **p**. *What it is that* **a** *does believe may be rather impenetrable. The root of the trouble may lie in anything from a minor piece of factual ignorance to an eccentric theory about the world, or even a radical confusion of thought.*

Thus propositions, like states of affairs, may be regarded as entities that are not fully determined, though in both cases and for many purposes we may properly act as though they were.

The idealised or Platonic picture which we are then using should not be attacked because it is idealised, any more than the idealisation involved in any scientific theory should render it open to suspicion. But idealisations need to be carefully handled. In this case, we should be taking the set of interchangeable sentences to which a proposition corresponds to be wholly determinate. The relation between sentence and proposition thus appears as analogous to the relation between token and type. Just as a class of tokens are tokens of the one type, so here a class of type sentences are expressions of the one proposition. And just as for many purposes it is appropriate to assume that it is determinate for any arbitrary token, whether or not it is a token of the one type, so it may be appropriate to assume that it is determinate for any arbitrary sentence whether or not it expresses a given proposition. But when the understanding of a sentence is in question, the class in which it is to be placed as expressing the same proposition is of course in question, so that it will be undetermined of certain sentences whether it is part of the way that a particular sentence is understood by someone that they should or should not be among the set of sentences taking which as interchangeable for the purpose at hand defines his understanding.

*Now in giving an outline of this position, we have apparently been led to
reinstate as a valid inference 'a believes* **p**; **p** *implies* **q***: therefore* **a** *believes*
q' *(among the possibly unwelcome consequences of which would be not only
that a person could not have an inconsistent belief, but that if he has a true
belief, then he believes all logical truths, and that if he has a false belief, then
he believes any proposition whatever). However, we have not committed
ourselves to its reinstatement. What we have done is to show that the reasons
sometimes advanced for holding the inference to be invalid, namely, the
alleged logical peculiarities of so-called intentional contexts, should be
dismissed. It is now open to us to consider any special features of notions such
as wanting and believing without the burdensome assumption that intentional contexts are logically anomalous.*

*It may indeed be found fruitful to formalise our findings, for instance by
appropriate definition of modal operators, but we are not obliged to do so in
order to escape intentional anomalies.*

*We shall not here engage in any substantial discussion of formalisations of
wants and beliefs, but some observations may appropriately be made. We
may hold, for instance, that wants that are inconsistent with each other, and
beliefs that are inconsistent with each other, can clearly coexist in the same
person; on the other hand, we may wish to deny the possibility of holding a
belief which is in itself inconsistent, or having a desire the specification of
whose object would include inconsistent propositions. In this way, we are
committing ourselves to the view that beliefs are to be distinguished from each
other, and wants too. (We should not accept the view on which it would in
the end be improper to treat different wants or beliefs as separable items rather
than as more or less arbitrarily isolated segments of the totality of a man's
wants or beliefs.) On the contrary, wants and beliefs are capable of
individuation (this is primarily a psychological task). Individual wants or
beliefs cannot be in themselves inconsistent (though the agent's attempted
treatment of a set of sentences as not involving inconsistency may show
confusion of thought on his part), but inconsistency may and does occur in the
set of wants or beliefs of a particular person. If we wish to represent these
views formally, we shall eliminate distribution in our rules for the modal
operators. In other words, we shall disallow the inference from 'a wants
(believes)* **p**' **&** '*a wants (believes)* **q**' *to* '*a wants (believes)* **p & q**'; *we
shall also disallow the inference from 'a wants* **p & q**' *to* '(*a wants* **p**) **&** (*a
wants* **q**)' *(though we may retain the inference from 'a wants* **p & q**' *to* '(*a
wants* **p**) **v** (*a wants* **q**)'. *Such a position will be developed, though not
formally, in section 2§4.*

But before we proceed to a more detailed consideration of wanting, a substantial objection to the whole procedure of this annex should be considered. It is conducted, we may hold, at the wrong level. Propositions and states of affairs are considered as entities, and—as if this were not bad enough—as unanalysed entities. On the contrary, it should be recognised that propositions only exist because of the terms which compose them, and states of affairs because of the objects which compose them. Thus any questions about the possibility or acceptability of treating propositions and states of affairs as entities must take second place to, or at the very least go along with, questions about the possibility or acceptability of treating terms and objects as entities.

This objection alone is decisive: it means that what has been said in this section cannot be treated as an adequate theory of propositions or of states of affairs. The crucial questions of their internal structure and of the possibility of reductivist accounts of them are left virtually untouched.

However, the purpose of this short section has not been to present such a theory, but rather, as was indicated at the outset, to say enough to make safe the use of the notions of propositions and states of affairs which it will be convenient to make in the account of wanting which is to follow.

And we have seen that it will be safe to use them so long as we bear in mind two provisos:

(1) we must fully recognise uncertainties in the identification of the propositions—and consequently the states of affairs—with which we are concerned (in particular, possible divergences between communally established understanding, and the—possibly confused—understanding of a particular person);

(2) we must consequently be ready to treat propositions and states of affairs as entities which are not fully determined.

These conditions may seem problematic, but they situate the problematic area where it is: neither in the perplexities of an outright Platonic transcendence, nor in the bleak theoretical landscape envisaged by the nominalist, but in the uncertainties of life, uncertainties which exist, both in the world, and in our response to it. To these responses we now return.

2 Wanting

§1. When a man has a desire, three conditions are satisfied. First, a description of some state of affairs in the form of a proposition or some conjunction of propositions will provide an answer to the question 'What does he want?'; secondly, this will be a description of a future state of affairs; and thirdly, the man will tend or intend to do something as tending to bring about that state of affairs. We may call these three criteria the *propositional*, the *prospective*, and the *conative*.

§2. It may seem that the propositional criterion does not always apply, since some desires are directed not upon states of affairs, but upon things. This is not so. Let Caroline want a rose. Upon what is her want directed? There need be no particular rose which she wants. In that case, what she wants is this: that the state of affairs in which she is in possession of some rose obtain, or that the proposition that for some rose she may be in possession of it be true. However, let us suppose that there is a particular rose—the one just out of reach on that bush—that she wants. Is it not then the case that what she wants is a thing, and not a state of affairs?

We ask here what would satisfy her desire. Would *that rose* satisfy it? In some way, certainly: but in what way? Would it satisfy her desire by remaining on the bush, by closing its petals, by being in her hand, by being in her dining-room, by being a gift offered to her, by changing colour? Caroline's desire cannot be satisfied by the rose as such (whatever that would be), but only by something being true of the rose.

A desire then is always directed upon some state of affairs; we can ascertain which one by asking what must happen to satisfy the desire. It is to be remarked that this question can in principle receive a definitive reply: that is, we can give a full specification of the state of affairs which would satisfy any desire by giving in full the propositions which the person who has the desire is (in respect of that desire) trying to make true. For instance, that I should pick the rose now and hand it to Caroline might be such a specification for her present desire. Notice that the state of affairs which is the object of desire is undetermined in all other respects, beyond those mentioned in the propositions given.

This may seem unsatisfactory: for I may make these propositions true while doing something that Caroline does *not* want. In picking the rose, I denude the bush; in handing it to Caroline, I thrust a thorn into her palm. She may want neither of these things. But then other conflicting desires have come into play.

It is important to notice here that there are two different cases of conflicting desires, the cases of extrinsic and of intrinsic conflict. As we have described our present example, the conflict between Caroline's desires might well be extrinsic in the one case, and intrinsic in the other.

An extrinsic conflict is one where no conflict emerges at the level of specifying the objects of desire: in other words, where the conflict occurs although we do not find incompatible propositions in those specifications. Here, we may say, the two desires just happen to come into conflict: indeed, it may be questioned whether conflict is an appropriate word at all. In our present example, Caroline had no reason to expect that receiving the rose would involve being hurt by the thorn. There is therefore (so far as we have stated the case) no reason to include not being pricked by the thorn in the specification of the original desire, and its conflict with the aversion to the pricking is extrinsic. (Note that aversions are treated as desires.)

An intrinsic conflict is one where conflict already emerges in the specification of the objects of desire, in that the specification of the one includes a proposition which is incompatible with a proposition included in the specification of the other. For example, Caroline may recognise that the picking of the rose in this case will denude the bush. And this may be unwelcome to her. Yet the description of the state of affairs which she wants in this case includes the proposition that the bush is denuded. We may wish to claim that since she does not want the bush denuded, this proposition cannot properly be included in the specification of any desire of hers. However, if she does take it that to have the rose handed to her is to have the bush denuded, then a description of the state of affairs which is her objective is incomplete if it excludes the denuding of the bush. Let her have other desires: for instance, that the description of whose object would include this—that the bush be left intact. These desires are in intrinsic conflict with the first precisely in that the specification of the one includes a proposition which is the negation of a proposition included in the specification of the other.

But now the claim that we can in principle give a full specification of the object of any desire looks much more problematic. Are we to include every proposition which the person whose desire is in question supposes will be true if his desire is fulfilled?

This question may best be answered as follows: when a person envisages and tries to bring about some state of affairs, he is concerning himself with a particular change in a relatively unchanging environment. A specification of the object of his desire will display that upon which his action is directed as distinguished from that which he will let be.

Of course, these limits to his field of action are notional: if he acts, there is no limit to the consequences, or alternatively, if he is to act, there will be no limit to the conditions to be fulfilled. This is the kind of dilemma often finding paradoxical expression in proverb and folklore (as, for instance, in the song 'There's a hole in my bucket'). Yet the same is true of the billiard ball in the classical model of causal action. It is only by an artificial and notional restriction that we consider the billiard table as a closed dynamic system. However, it is a fruitful simplification of a kind indispensable in the sciences, though the modes of simplification or idealisation call for careful scrutiny, as will be argued in section 13 below. Correspondingly, the boundaries that a person tacitly draws round his field of action, though they may be less clear cut, and much more changeable, are equally indispensable to his activity. In reality, he acts in the universe as a whole—and he knows it; but he can only know what he is doing, he can only act, by making the defeasible assumption that the field of possibilities within which his action will take place is effectively closed.

Thus the first boundary we find around a person's desire is a boundary determining the set of propositions whose truth-value is taken to be fixed by the accomplishment of that desire, and distinguishing them from those whose truth-value is taken not to be so fixed. Note that this distinction is determined by what the person whose desire is in question takes to be the case: he may of course be mistaken—the accomplishment of his desire may in fact fix the truth-value of propositions outside that boundary. It is also possible, as we shall see shortly, for it to fix the truth-value of propositions within the boundary in the 'wrong' direction.

But first let us consider the distinction in more detail. It is clear for some cases. If we return to Caroline, that the bush be denuded is a proposition which, she takes it, would be fixed as true by the accomplishment of her desire for the rose. But, for instance, the proposition that her brother will miss his breakfast the following morning is not so fixed.

However, the matter is less clear if we consider what may be called *background conditions*. A person will take it that there is a range of conditions (from general physical laws to more specific circumstances) without which his desire could not be accomplished. In that case, if the desire is accomplished, the truth of the propositions stating those conditions is fixed. On the other hand, we may object that the truth of such propositions is not fixed *by* the event in question. And the idea behind this objection is that the truth of the law of gravity, for instance, is not contingent upon the human will. The objection may be reinforced by appealing once more to the idea of the boundaries drawn—and unavoidably drawn—by a person around his 'field of action'. Surely, he will not draw them so as to include conditions of this kind.

But this objection is question-begging. And it seems to me that conditions of this kind are to be included, for the accomplishment of a person's desire would indeed be taken by him to fix as true such background conditions (without being taken to bring about their truth: what is brought about is the state of affairs designated by the whole set of propositions). Of course, for many purposes, these background conditions can be ignored. They will recur, in various combinations, for many different desires, for the same person or for others. They are therefore able to be cancelled out, or treated as a kind of fixed framework for action, as the Newtonian laws of motion, together with the various special forces, would provide a framework for the action of the billiard balls.

If we share a person's assumptions about background conditions, we shall be all the more inclined to set them on one side, and not to include them in the specification of any desire of his. But they cannot in general be set aside for the following reason. The sets of propositions which specify the objects of desire have it as their function to indicate what a person is trying to bring about. If his assumptions about the background conditions are different from ours, we shall not know what he is trying to bring about, if we have omitted them from the specifications. This may be especially obvious in the case of the desires of a 'mentally disordered' person, or of a person from a radically different culture.

Thus 'background' conditions are to be included in the specification of objects of desire. But this raises a further problem. Not only have these specifications now become extremely unwieldy:

they also seem to include propositions performing two quite different roles—those which, as we might say, really indicate what the person is after, and those which merely give the person's views of the accompanying conditions.

This is the distinction which we shall later consider in more detail between the essential and the non-essential occurrence of a proposition in the specification of an object of desire. Putting it briefly, a proposition is said to occur non-essentially when the desire which it helps to specify would still be considered to be fulfilled even if, contrary to expectation, that proposition were not made true by the accomplishment of the desire. This is one way, as we said earlier, in which a person may be mistaken in the boundary he draws around his field of action.

Now the constant reference in what has been argued here to what a subject *takes* to be so, and the very terminology of propositions, may suggest an account of desire which would require in the wanter conscious and specific mental acts of entertaining propositions and considering their consequences. In fact, of course, the proposition which is the complete specification of an object of desire need not at any point be consciously entertained by an agent. It may be merely implicit in his thoughts or in his behaviour; and it may remain partially provisional or indeterminate until the moment of completion. So the basic thrust of this interpretation of wanting—that it should be seen as the attempt to match the world to a blueprint—should not be crudely translated into the substantial (and bizarre) psychological thesis that whenever a man wants something his first step is to go through the intellectual process of framing certain propositions—of preparing and inspecting a blue-print.

§3. The second condition satisfied when a man has a desire is that the set of propositions specifying the object of his desire apply to a future state of affairs. It may seem that this condition does not always hold since a person may desire what is already the case. For instance, a man might want the company of a friend while already in his company. But what is in fact wanted here is that the meeting should continue, and the continuance of a present state of affairs is of course in the future. A person does not want what he already has. But I may be mistaken. I may be ignorant of the fact that the state of affairs which I am after already obtains. Let us say that my picking of the rose is intended to placate Caroline after my bad behaviour yesterday. But this placating, this attempt to make her once more well-disposed towards me, is superfluous. She does not need placating. The desired state of affairs already exists.

But of course we have not held that the set of propositions specifying an object of desire will be true only in the future. Rather, for a person to have that desire is for him to treat that set of propositions as denoting a future state which he would try to bring about.

§ 4. This leads us to the third criterion of wanting—that the man is treating some proposition as something to be realised, that he tends or intends to do something as tending to bring about the state of affairs he has in mind.

Notice that this criterion implies the first two criteria. If, then, it can be treated by itself as a necessary and sufficient condition for a case of wanting, it seems to follow, if we grant that everything a person does, *a fortiori* he tends or intends to do, that a person never does anything that he doesn't want to do.

Is this conclusion tolerable? Suppose that Caroline and I are in a public park. I do not want to pick flowers in such a place, but still I pick the rose for Caroline when she makes it clear that she wants it. Can I not say that though I did want to please her, I did not want to pick the flower? Here we have once more the distinction between propositions that occur essentially and propositions which do not occur essentially in the specification of a desire. Let us take it that the propositions that I am trying to make true here are at least the following: that I should pick this rose in this public park, that I should hand it to Caroline, and that I should thereby please her. Let us further suppose that if Caroline were not pleased, my desire would not be satisfied: in that case, the proposition that she should be pleased by the gesture occurs essentially in the specification of the object of my desire. If, on the other hand, the first proposition turns out to be false, because the place is not a public park at all, and if in spite of this I should still take my desire to have been accomplished, then the first proposition does not occur essentially in the specification of the object of my desire.

In general, if *a desires* (p & q & r), we cannot infer that (*a desires p*) and (*a desires q*) and (*a desires r*); we can however infer that (*a desires p*) or (*a desires q*) or (*a desires r*), for at least one of the propositions specifying the object of his desire must occur essentially (in other words, it could not be the case that someone had a certain desire, and that it was satisfied, when *none* of the propositions in the set specifying the object of desire was true).

Thus we should not claim that what a person does is always what he wants to do, but more carefully that the proposition(s) describing the state of affairs which he takes himself to be bringing about must be included in or must include the set of propositions which specify a state of affairs which he wants, even though the proposition(s) describing the state of affairs which he takes himself to be bringing about may not occur essentially in the specification of the object of that desire, and even though they may even be included in or include the specification of the object of some conflicting desire.

In this way, we can give a better account of the cases in which a person says of his own action that he did not want to do it; for we see now that though its description must overlap the specification of some want of his, it need not coincide; and where it does not coincide, such a description would not rightly be taken as the specification of a want at all: indeed, it may enter into the specification of a conflicting want.

Now in dealing with this first difficulty about the conative criterion, we were led to say that what a person does, *a fortiori* he tends or intends to do. And it may seem that two important questions are begged here: first, how do we distinguish actions from mere movements? (For there would arguably be no such *a fortiori* if 'unwilled movements' of a person's body were to be included in what he is said to do.) Secondly, it is clear (and here tacitly supposed) that a tendency or intention to act may exist without coming to fruition. Then what does such a tendency or intention consist in?

Tendencies exist as states of being actually and actively directed towards some future state of affairs. When accompanying the accomplishment of that goal, they constitute its being willed. In saying this, we bypass current controversies concerning the relation between intention and action, and whether it could be causal; we ignore traditional epistemological questions about how I can know what my intention is, or how another can know; and we offer no means of distinguishing the 'tendencies or intentions' to act with which we are concerned from activities of autonomous systems, for instance in the human body, which show the same formal pattern, but are not 'subject to the will'. Consider for example the homeostatic regulation of the blood sugar level. It would be correct to say that this mechanism is in a 'state of being actually and actively directed towards a future state of affairs'.

In ignoring all these questions, we are effectively treating the notions of a tendency or intention to act, and of the attribution of a change to such a tendency, as primitive. It may seem perverse, even though all explanation must start somewhere, to take as a starting-point what has traditionally been a major point of philosophical debate. But that appearance of perversity is perhaps attributable to philosophy's preoccupation with the special place of man, and hence of itself, in the order of things. Questions about the specific character of human willing are more properly attacked in biology, cybernetics, psychology, general systems theory, sociology, or even physics, than in philosophy. These are points to which we shall briefly return in section 13. For the present, we shall openly refuse an answer to these questions, and stipulate the notions in question as primitive.

But given that we have done this, a third difficulty arises for the conative criterion for wanting. It may seem that the strong connection established between wanting and acting would leave us unable to deal with the case of conflicting wants. For if one of the wants is not acted on (as must be the case), how on the present account can it be a want at all?

Consider a case. The park-keeper, in our interview after the plucking of the rose, begins to eye Caroline in an offensive manner. I hesitate for a moment, having two conflicting wants—one to placate him and avoid further fuss over the rose, and the other to rebuke his offence. Then I rebuke him. Note that throughout the interview and the moment of hesitation, I wanted to placate the keeper. That is, I did have a real tendency to placate the man at least until the moment of rebuke. Thus although two (practically or logically) incompatible actions cannot both be performed, nevertheless two *tendencies* which are tendencies to perform incompatible actions can coexist. Indeed, the existence of such tendencies to act independent of the actions in which they may (or may not) issue, is, as already remarked, an important part of the position being proposed.

But this case of conflicting desires raises the question of their strength or intensity. What account can we give of such variations between desires? An important dimension of the answer is closed to us here, for, as we shall admit and justify in annex (v) below, the present account of desires takes no account of their affective aspects—of their embodiment. As yet we have only partially relaxed the abstractions which enabled us to construct the model universe of section 1. In this case, it must be granted that the intensity of a desire may exist and be felt in the body: there is yearning in the bowels. But I would maintain that differences in the strength of desires do not consist in such sensations: they consist in different degrees of readiness to combat difficulties and obstacles to their fulfilment. And this readiness is itself an aspect of the tendencies to action of which we have spoken.

But what of cases where no action is open? Can a man not have a desire (even a strong desire), and yet be powerless, and believe himself to be powerless, to further it in any way? May I not long to fall in love, or want a fine day? This possibility constitutes a serious objection to the conative criterion for wanting, and will be considered in section 3.

(iv) Paronymy

But before we discuss the relation between wishing and wanting, it is necessary to consider a problem in the theory of meaning.

Sometimes the same term is applied to different things because they satisfy the same criteria; this is the case in which Aristotle used the term **synonymy**. *Sometimes, however, the same term is applied to different things although the criteria of application of the term in the different cases are quite unrelated; this is the case in which Aristotle used the term* **homonymy**. *One intermediary case is discussed by Aristotle himself—the case in which the same term is applied to different things by an indirect appeal to the same criteria (as a food, a climate, a complexion, and a man may all be called 'healthy' in virtue of their different relations to the one notion of health in a man—* πρὸς ἓν λεγόμενον). *Another intermediary case is that in which the things are called by the same term because each of them satisfies a sufficient number of a set of criteria (though there may be little overlap between the criteria actually satisfied in any pair of cases); this is the case where Wittgenstein spoke of 'family resemblances'.*

But there is a further kind of intermediary case—where things are called alike because they are deemed to satisfy the same criteria. This is the case in which I wish to use the term **paronymy** *and of which I now offer some examples. (Note that this application of the term is different from that assigned to it by Aristotle at the beginning of the De Interpretatione.)*

Consider the following regulation: 'A resident is any person who has resided continuously in the country for at least the six months immediately preceding the date of his application: except that persons who have left the country only for short periods during those six months may be deemed resident.' Here two classes of people are (rightly) called residents: those who satisfy a certain criterion, and those who do not satisfy it but are deemed to.

Again, when children play families, the one may call the other mother, though his 'mother' does not satisfy the criteria by which a person is properly so-called, when for the purposes of the game she is deemed to satisfy them.

These are merely examples, and the notion of 'deeming' which they illustrate is in need of explication. We have already in annex (iii) advanced reasons for holding in the case of sentence-meaning that outside a central common domain where a Platonic extrapolation of propositions with strict identity is made, other domains such as those defined by beliefs, wants and modalities must be taken as disposing propositions with weak criteria of identity. As we have noted, this would emerge at the level of terms in the form of weakened (trans-world) identity criteria for the individuals in the worlds of belief, desire and so forth. We now have a corresponding thesis about predicates, for predicates in two 'worlds' may be analogous. Take the case of the children's game. Here the children create and people an imaginary world of a simplified kind based on some of their experiences of the real world. Now the girl who plays mother is not 'in fact' a mother: but she is a mother in the world of the game. Certain roles and attributes are assigned to her, and for the purpose of the game, so long as it is being played, she will be the mother. She is not improperly (homonymously) so-called, nor is she so-called for the same reasons as real mothers (synonymously): purposes at hand have established a recognisable and delimited context within which the predicate 'mother' is applied to her in virtue of criteria other than those in virtue of which it is regularly or primarily applied. One may say: 'because that is what it is to be a mother in a game.'

Consider also the example of the regulation: the person affected by it may not in law be a resident, but the regulation itself (as administered by certain officials in the light of certain other practices and regulations, and as having a certain range of consequences when applied) itself establishes a delimited context within which a person who is not a resident may parony-mously—and properly—be called a resident.

Consider also Joule's experiment. In this experiment, a beaker of water is taken, and a paddle operable by a falling weight attached to it through a gearing and pulley system is immersed in the water. When the weight is raised, the system has a certain (potential) energy. The problem raised by Joule was this: if the weight is allowed to fall, that potential energy is lost from the system; hence the experiment constitutes a refutation of the principle of the conservation of energy. Joule's solution was to recognise heat as a form of energy. Then we find in his experiment that the movement of the paddle heats the water, and we are able to retain the principle of the conservation of energy.

Now before Joule, the term 'energy' was applied (in scientific contexts) in virtue of the mass and velocity of bodies: its primary application was therefore to moving bodies. An extension to stationary bodies becomes possible by allowing, for instance, a certain potential velocity to a suspended body in virtue of what will happen to it when released, or equivalently in virtue of the energy required in suspending it.

But on what grounds could heat be regarded as a form of energy? Joule's *experiment provided an experimental and scientific context in which it was reasonable and fruitful to deem heat to be a form of energy even though at that time, and for a long time, scientists lacked that development of physical theory which would justify Joule's extension of 'energy' to include heat by showing how the term could be applied to both cases in virtue of the very same criteria. Pending that advance, there were on the one hand the cases of 'energy' which satisfied the conventional criterion, and on the other the cases of heat, which were thought not to, but were none the less deemed to. To make use of this insight, it was necessary to adopt, as Joule did, a quantified principle of equivalence between the two kinds of energy, which was arbitrary in so far as it had no theoretical backing, but justified in so far as it worked.*

There is a further question: what made it reasonable to regard the new principle as a principle of the conservation of 'energy'? After all, heat simply was not energy in the received sense. Why not deem energy to be a form of heat? Or why not hold that both energy and heat are manifestations of some third phenomenon? The answer seems to lie in what may be called the theoretical geography of the principle of the conservation of energy (here, and throughout this section, there is an appeal to metaphor to give an account of a notion of metaphor: for a scientific principle and a watershed do not synonymously have a geographical position: there is a problem here which will be reverted to briefly at the end of this annex). The received principle played a certain role in the context of mechanical systems as conventionally envisaged. The new principle will play a closely analogous role with respect to systems in which heat too is involved. Such structural similarity or homology is what justifies regarding the new principle as a principle of the conservation of energy. For the time being, heat is properly, but only paronymously, called energy.

Thus, in general, predicates with a primary application in one domain may acquire secondary applications in other domains according to the purposes defining those domains. It is such secondary applications of a predicate that are sometimes marked by the idioms of deeming, and which we here characterise as 'paronymous'.

However, this account of paronymy raises major problems: first, it has inescapably itself been established by the use of some strategic paronymies, such as that of a 'domain', and such as that of being in an 'intermediate' position on a scale whose limits are homonymy and synonymy. Secondly, it has been an important feature of the notion of paronymy here advanced that terms used paronymously can nevertheless be properly so used. There is an appearance of paradox here, for we should commonly mark a non-paronymous use as proper. But the aim must be to make possible a distinction between those transfers of a term from one domain to another which are appropriate, justified, fruitful, correct, and those which are not.

The only way of establishing such a distinction that has been hinted at in our present discussion is a form of pragmatism. It was said, for instance, that Joule's principle of equivalence 'worked'. This can only mean that it was a device which enabled scientists to generate a wider variety of true non-paronymous statements. The paronymous form of the principle of the conservation of energy only became directly justifiable with the establishment of the molecular theory of heat. But at this point, precisely, the term 'energy' ceased to be paronymous in its application to heat. For in a wide range of cases heat was now literally a matter of the movement of particles—of mass and velocity. What were two domains linked by a strategic paronymy have now decisively merged into one.

However, this pragmatic or instrumentalist solution is really an evasion. Although it gives a justification for using a paronymous expression, it does not give an account of that in which the appropriateness of the paronymy consists.

We need, therefore, a solution such as that hinted at above in paronymous terms, namely that the paronymy is appropriate in proportion to the structural similarity between the position of the term in its own domain, and its position in the domain where it is to have its paronymous application—in proportion, that is, to an ascertainable homology between two predicates in two domains.

This is a line of solution which raises too many problems to be developed usefully here, but let us allow that it gives enough substance to the notion of paronymy to allow us to use it in what follows. The problems will recur in section 13. Meanwhile, let us consider the nature of wishing.

3 Wishing

Wanting has been defined by three criteria, the *conative* (there being a tendency to action), the *prospective* (the action being directed at bringing about what is believed to be a possible future state of affairs), and the *propositional* (the state of affairs being designated by a set of propositions).

Now human engagement in the world is not purely practical, that is, restricted to the consideration and implementation of what can in fact be done. Imagination, for example, is a faculty by which we can take pleasure or refuge in the contemplation of the unattainable, or in the pretence of its attainment. However, the distinction between the real world and the world of the imagination needs to be taken carefully. Certainly, the world of a novel, for instance, is imaginary: yet the world of, say, *Middlemarch* is by no means unrelated to the real world of nineteenth-century English society. Moreover, our attitudes towards what passes in that imaginary world are by no means unrelated to our attitudes towards what passes in the real world. Furthermore, imaginary worlds sometimes come into being. What begins in play may end in life. Or indeed, what begins in life may be transmuted into a relived dream.

We may return for a moment to what was said in section 2 above about an agent's delimitation of his field of action. This delimitation may be more or less realistic. The man may subtly or grossly modify his purchase on the world: he may, for all kinds of motives from experimental curiosity to pathological fear, modify his map of what is and of what is possible—and this is also to modify the kinds of actions open to him, even to the extreme point at which nothing resembling an 'ordinary action' is open at all, so that all that is left to the agent is to go through a kind of magical charade, a ritual which may be experienced as the natural expression of the 'desire' in mild cases, or may be pursued with passion in extreme cases as though it were an attempt actually to bring about the desired goal.

It should not be thought that the first step outside a severe pragmatic view of one's field of action is a step into pathology. For there is in any case no single or clear criterion to determine a particular boundary delimiting a field of action as discussed in section 2 above as normal, pragmatic or rational. Anomalies may enter from the moment at which any boundary at all is drawn. But as we have seen, action is impossible without such boundaries. This is man's predicament: at the same time his will is not master of the entire universe, and on the other hand there are no closed and predetermined limits to its exercise: so our boundaries may be ambitious or cautious, closed or permeable, fixed or shifting, and so forth.

It is on these complex boundaries that the notions of wishing and wanting range. A stern distinction between the two worlds would lead to a sharp distinction between the cases where, it is held, we can and do try to get something, and the other cases in which we have set ourselves unrealistic goals, but English idiom, unlike that of some other languages, such as French, is less strict. For we do sometimes regard ourselves as *wanting* what we cannot get, and do not believe ourselves able to get.

This idiomatic point is rather instructive: where in English the homology between a 'realistic' and an 'unrealistic' desire is marked by using the same term in both cases, in French we use the same verb but in 'unrealistic' cases it appears in the conditional tense. Thus in French we assume the practicability of a distinction between the central cases where there is a real tendency to action (and where we may use the verb *vouloir* in tenses other than the conditional), and the other cases where there is what *would be* such a tendency if it were possible (and here we use *vouloir* in the conditional tense). The distinction between the English *wanting* and *wishing* is analogous, save that wanting is allowed greater scope. In what follows, it will be convenient to mark the distinction between cases where there is a real tendency to action and cases where there is not as a distinction between wishing and wanting, and it is in this sense that we shall henceforth use these terms.

Now what is the relation between wishing and wanting? A first attempt at an answer might have been to claim that whereas cases of wanting satisfy the three criteria already suggested, cases of wishing satisfy only the first two of these criteria. This, however, would be insufficient: for wishing is more than merely envisaging a state of affairs and taking it to be in the future. It is, after all, what has pallidly been called a 'pro-attitude'. What then in the case of wishes constitutes their directedness towards the desired goal?

Let us take a clue from the French conditional idiom noticed above.

We may start by attempting the following account. A person wishes *p* if and only if he would want *p*. But 'would want' under what conditions? Presumably that some action were open to him in the matter. We now say that if an action is open and the man has a tendency to perform it, then he wants *p*; while if no action is open, but if there were a suitable action the man would have a tendency to perform it, then he wishes *p*.

But this account is unsatisfactory for many reasons. Consider a person of sternly pragmatic temperament—one who does not harbour many wishes. Now consider any situation such that from our knowledge of the man, we can be sure that if any action were open to him, he would tend to take it, to achieve a certain goal. For instance, he sees some artichokes in the shop, but has no money in his pocket. We can be sure from our knowledge of his tastes and habits that if he had some money he would have a tendency to buy some. In that case, on the suggested account of wishing it would be a matter of definition that he now wishes for some artichokes. This is clearly unsatisfactory. It may be the case that a person would want *p* and that he does not wish *p*.

Let us then follow the clue of conditionality in another way: a person wishes *p* if and only if he does what would be wanting *p* if the conditions allowed it. In this case, we suppose in the wisher some substitute for or analogue of the tendency to action which occurs in wanting: we suppose that some predicate homologous to 'ξ wants p' is true of him. Consider the boy who repeatedly telephones the girl who will have no more of him. The actions that he performs (and the tendencies to perform them) are of course perfectly real, considered in themselves. But they are notionally aimed at a re-establishment of the boy's relations with the girl, which, in the case we are imagining, he sees no way of achieving, though he yearns for it—he wishes it. The telephone calls are not genuine attempts to achieve a goal, but they are expressions of his yearning, since they are at least notionally, at least in an imaginary world, directed towards that goal. The daydream that the right words spoken into the mouthpiece will heal the breach is real, but not realistic.

Of course, there is a certain oversimplification involved in our account of this case, even given the way in which we have set it up. For who can say that the right words would not have the desired effect, even though the boy may be sure in his heart that he will not find them? In other words, in an actual case like the one described, it would not be as unequivocal a case of 'wishing' as we have tended to suggest. Suppose one of his 'phone calls is successful, and the girl relents. It is not clear how he will react, and this may be left indeterminate in his present wish/want. If he is frightened and paralysed by this success, not knowing what to do in a situation which was quite unexpected, we shall be inclined to treat him as having a mere wish, belonging to a well-insulated imaginary world. If on the other hand he immediately takes advantage of her relenting, enthusiastically but practically, surprised but not disturbed by it, then we shall be inclined to think of him as having entertained a want—long shot though it may have been and seemed. A continuous range of cases may lie between these two extremes.

But so far we have considered only a case of wishing in which the actions and tendencies to action, though unrealistic in their goal, are nevertheless real actions with only a tinge of ritual. There are cases, however, where the ritual gesture is the only available expression of the wish, like the man at the railway station whose gesture of outstretched arms at the departing train may be paronymously pulling the train back to prevent his separation from a lover.

We have now made explicit what was implicit earlier in this section: namely, the importance of the notion of paronymy discussed in annex (iv) above. By it we are enabled to express our account of wishing as follows: whereas in the case of wanting, the propositional, the prospective and the conative criteria are all satisfied; in the case of wishing, the first two criteria are satisfied, but the third only paronymously.

But there seems to be a further artificiality here. For the requirement of the prospective criterion excludes wishes directed upon the past or the present, although idiomatically there are such wishes. Indeed, the English idiom 'wish that' never takes a straight future tense; this is reserved for the case of 'making a wish'. This is indeed precisely the purest example of the class of cases for which it will be convenient to reserve the term *wishing*. The other cases fall under a different category to be considered in section 4.

(v) Abstraction

But first let it be noted that the analysis so far offered is achieved by a sort of phenomenological abstraction of the body. Thus while we have indeed moved some way back to this world from the model universe of section 1, the account is still proceeding at a certain level of abstraction. In fact, though any desire does satisfy our three conditions, and though these conditions are necessary and sufficient, yet because we are embodied (and it is not to our present purpose to discuss the possibility of a disembodied existence), our desires are characteristically lived through and in the body, and the yearnings in the bowels which may supervene have been excluded from our account.

It is important to bear this in mind, since the abstraction is much more noticeable in the case of the third variation which we are going on to discuss, where an account will be offered of pleasures. For bodily sensations are often the most notable aspect of pleasures. Nevertheless we shall maintain the abstraction of the affective in order to draw attention to the links between wanting and wishing on the one hand, and pleasures on the other, since the nature of these links is central to our argument, and easily obscured by urgent sensation.

4 Pleasure

We have so far considered two modalities of the pure will of section I in the case of human agents—*wanting* and *wishing*. But there is a third modality. Whereas the second satisfies the three criteria for wanting save that in the passage to 'imaginary worlds' the conative criterion is only paronymously satisfied, in the case of the third modality, the prospective criterion also is only paronymously satisfied.

The conative attitudes with which we started (wanting) were at home in the world of the attainable. When we turned to what is beyond the attainable, however, we found a set of cognate attitudes (wishing). What will happen when we turn to what is on this side of the attainable—to what is already attained? What when what is *to be attained* is neither attainable (something we want), nor beyond the attainable (something we wish for), but something which is attained already? Here, I argue, we have a further set of cognate attitudes, of which the characteristic example is taking pleasure in a thing. Taking pleasure is what would be wanting, but that what is wanted is already present.

We have here an explanation of that supervenience of pleasure to which Aristotle drew attention in another way. For the appetite produced by the pleasurable situation (and which constitutes its being pleasurable) has no function, since that which it is the tendency to strive for is already present. So a desire may be awakened by the advent of the very situation for which it should be the desire. This superfluous desire, this purely paronymous striving for a present situation which is through that striving only paronymously treated as being in prospect, naturally overflows into the smiles, the deep breaths, the expansive gestures which form a happy charade of striving for that which has been vouchsafed from the first. Such is pleasure.

(vi) Perfect Peace

We have now the outlines of a map of human appetite: a monochromatic map, since we have left out of account the fact that man has a body. But there are two main features of man which are held constant in this map. First, that feature of man which is captured by calling him a rational being: it is a feature which emerges in our map in the production of propositions to which the world may be matched, or against which it may be measured; secondly, man appears in our map as an essentially active being.

We may instructively ask what lies beyond our map at these points. In other words, what lies beyond the boundary of propositions, and what lies beyond the boundary of activity?

It seems that beyond the boundary of propositions lies the animal world. For at best we can only paronymously attribute the entertainment of propositions to animals; yet we cannot avoid thinking of them and treating them as having at least some desires. We descry at once a whole further area linked to the original ground which we have surveyed in sections 2—4 above by another strategic paronymy, that according to which animals are properly but paronymously said to be trying to make certain propositions true. However, it will not be part of our present task to explore this area.

Up to this point we have considered a number of modes of the will, each new mode linked to the central case by a strategic paronymy. And the central thread throughout is the presence of some form of activity. Yet do not some pleasures call into question the primacy of the will? Man may be an active being: in that case, he does not know 'what to do' when confronted with the unlooked for and unworked for fulfilment of desires that he has not even had the time to formulate: hence we have claimed that his pleasure is his treating that situation, as best he can, as an object of desire.

Yet why should he be held in a trap of ceaseless activity, especially when activity is superfluous? This question should lead us to acknowledge what is obvious: that the present account of pleasure cannot be regarded as more than a foothold on very difficult terrain. It is not a primary purpose of the main argument to develop a theory of pleasure, and it would be absurd to think that a few words would suffice for this. Thus, though the few words of section 4 may strictly suffice for the main argument, we shall not here leave them entirely without support or development.

35

*It is in the first place rather easy to discern a development which would enable us to deal with displeasure and similar phenomena. For just as avoidance may be assimilated to wanting (by treating it as wanting not-*p*), so displeasures can be interpreted within the framework of the existing account of pleasures as the presence of a tendency to bring it about that not-*p*, which is idle just to the extent that it is too late to bring it about that now not-*p* when* p *already now obtains. Such a move becomes problematic, however, in the case of pain, since it omits an essential: pain as a sensation. Moreover, the same difficulty already confronts us in the case of pleasurable sensations. We have, it is true, already adverted to, and given some justification of, our abstraction of the body, but it may still be held that there are cases, such as sexual pleasure, in which the account given cannot stand, since embodiment is an essential feature of such pleasures, which are at least in part irreducibly a matter of sensation, rather than of an attitude towards some sensation.*

This objection seems to me sound, in that it shows that not everything that can reasonably be considered to be a pleasure can be directly accounted for by our account of 'pleasure'; and parallel considerations apply to pain. There is, however, a strategy for dealing with these cases which takes rise from the general structure of the argument presented. For we have already referred to a world of animal desire generated by the paronymous application of the propositional criterion to animals. Now man too is an animal. And in the animal world we find the physiological correlates of desire, hitherto defined in non-physiological terms. Thus physiological phenomena, say of the organism 'striving towards' ejaculation, or showing aversion from a painful stimulus, are formally homologous (in terms of the applicability of our three criteria) to the non-paronymous causes of wanting, of which the subject is a person, and not a purely organic entity.

Yet it is not clear how this observation can help us. We may grant animals wants, and allow even physiological processes to be paronymously so classified. But how can this help us with animal pleasures? If the paronymous shift is consistently made, a pleasure in this animal world would be an excess animal appetite, a superfluous physiological striving for an already existing condition. That this abstract possibility is not merely speculative will be indicated in section 13 below. However, even ignoring the problem of the gap between a physiological event and a sensation, it seems clear that such an account would be at best insufficient to deal, for instance, with the case cited of sexual pleasure. For this case, quite apart from the essential involvement of sensation, has two important features not captured in our account: first, that of pleasurable activity, and second the pleasure of satisfied desire.

Now activity becomes problematic for us to the extent that it may be its own end, that in doing it, the agent has no end beyond doing it. In our account not only of pleasure, but also of wanting and wishing, we have in fact taken as our examples of objects of desire only states (such as being in possession of a rose), and not activities (such as digging the flower bed). It is true that nothing in our appeal to the notion of states of affairs excludes activities; but the problem arises from this—that whereas in the cases hitherto cited there is a ready distinction between the actions or activities which manifest a desire and the state of affairs which is its accomplishment, we now have cases where that distinction does not exist. Consider the desire to be playing squash. Certainly, this desire can be manifested in just the same way as others which we have considered: for before the game, the player will find another person to play with, collect his equipment, see to it that there is an available squash court, and so forth. But is not his desire to play also, and indeed pre-eminently, manifested in his actually playing? That which above all brings it about that he is playing is that he is playing. Here is an activity which may be considered an accomplishment of its own end. Such an example differs from cases of wanting, under our definition, in that the prospective criterion does not apply (not even paronymously); but it differs from pleasures, under our definition, in that the conative criterion does apply non-paronymously. That is, the activity which is the object of the person's present desire is not taken to be in the future (so that we do not seem to have a case of wanting, as here defined); while on the other hand the tendency or intention to act in the matter is really and not just paronymously present.

Thus whereas our account is generated on the basis of the primary case of wanting in which there is a gap between desire and possible fulfilment (the prospective criterion applies), now we see a further dimension of variation produced by dropping the prospective criterion—cases of 'wanting' in which striving collapses into achievement. What would pleasures be along this dimension? The following strategy may be suggested: we shall appeal to an awareness in the agent not only of the coincidence of his activity considered as an object of desire with his activity considered as producing that object; but in addition of their coincidence with that which would be a striving for that state of affairs or activity, were it not present. In short, just as there is a variety of wanting in which the goal and the action directed towards it collapse into each other, so there is a variety of pleasure in which the 'extra' paronymous striving which characterises more central cases of pleasure collapses into the activity itself. This then would be a strategy for exploring what may lie behind Aristotle's metaphor for pleasure in an activity, that it is like 'the bloom of youth'.

But at the opposite limit to that of pleasurable activity, there seems to be the pleasure of satisfied desire, where no additional paronymous desire is excited. In other words, though not all satisfaction of desires need be *pleasurable, yet in some cases we do find an essentially tranquil pleasure which again does not conform to our main account of pleasures. We now envisage the granting or attaining of a state of complete tranquillity, a state in which desire (including that mode of it which we have called pleasure) would have been quite transcended—the state of perfect peace.*

That there must be an end of all striving, and that it must be a state of tranquillity (in which there is no striving for goals) has been a persistent theme in moral speculation from Aristotle's somewhat sophistical arguments that the state or activity of intellectual contemplation—of θεωρία—is the aim of all aims, to the arcana of religious mysticism.

We shall have occasion to revert to this topic in section 13. Meanwhile, with these brief observations on strategies for developing the theory so far advanced (particularly in respect of its application to pleasure), we shall review our conclusions up to this point.

5 Appetitives

What we have so far observed is a common structure in a wide variety of different psychological situations. The whole class of cases considered may be called *appetitives*, since they all involve some form of (real or paronymous) striving for some state of affairs.

The primary sort of appetitive is the *conative* in which all three conditions of section 2 hold. This is the case of which wanting is the paradigmatic example. But, of course, wanting in the sense defined is a feature of many different psychological states. The analysis adumbrated will enable us to display what may be called the appetitive skeleton of all such cases. We may instance looking for (wanting to find), being curious about (wanting to know about), loving (wanting to benefit, to be with, etc.), competing (wanting to defeat), hating (wanting to destroy), attacking (wanting to render innocuous), being ambitious (wanting to advance oneself).

Alongside conatives are the two cognate branches of the family of appetitives: *optatives* (cases in which the conative criterion is satisfied only paronymously and of which wishes are paradigmatic), and *fruitives* (cases in which both the conative and the prospective criteria are satisfied only paronymously and of which pleasures are paradigmatic). Optatives would include, for instance, cases of despair, anxiety, anticipation; fruïtives—pride, regret, admiration. Alongside this family are the families of *animal appetitives* (where the propositional criterion is satisfied only paronymously), and *energetic appetitives* (where the prospective criterion is not satisfied), both adumbrated in annex (vi) above.

However, it must be remarked that a particular psychological state need not necessarily fall under only one of these categories. A particular case of admiration, for example, might include a conative component (wanting to imitate), an optative component (wishing to be the other person), and a fruïtive component (taking a particular pleasure in the fact that such a person exists). Animal appetitives too might be in play. Moreover, there is no once for all appetitive analysis of all cases to which we apply a term such as 'admiration'.

In fact, the analysis would enable us to disengage certain complexities in any particular situation according to rather simple general principles. Thus the 'appetitive skeleton' which it enables us to display is not the skeleton of, for instance, ambition or admiration in general, but of any particular case of these or other psychological postures. The application of this analysis would be a matter of psychological practice.

My purpose here is not to carry out such an applied investigation, but to base a theory of value on the possibility of carrying it out.

(vii) Ends and Means

But there is a difficulty to be confronted before we turn to values. For are
not the specifications of the objects of appetitives which we have discussed at
length specifications of ends? What of the means? Nothing has been said, it
may be held, about the adoption of means to those ends, about the ways in
which those ends can provide reasons for acting, or act as motives. In short,
the operation of what since Aristotle has been called 'practical reason' has
been left out of account. This omission is serious enough in the area of
theoretical psychology to which the main argument has up to now been
confined. It will become unacceptable if it is carried over to the theory of
value.

The brief answer to this difficulty is that the propositions specifying the
objects of appetitives are precisely not Aristotelian major premises in a
practical syllogism. We are not dealing here with relatively independent
psychological forces or entities postulated in such a way that they open up as
the main topic of enquiry the links between them and any actions which may
issue. On the contrary, a want as we have defined it is a tendency to act in
certain ways with a certain end in view. Consequently, the connections
which are the concern of practical reason belong within the structure of the
objects of appetitives. The reason for an action, or its motive, the end and the
means, these things must appear in a full statement of what it is that a person
wants in acting in such and such a way. In effect, then, these questions are just
some of the many different kinds of question that can be asked about the way
in which a particular proposition occurs in the specification of the object of an
appetitive.

A first important distinction is one already noticed, that between the
essential and non-essential occurrence of a proposition in such specifications.
Starting from this distinction, we find approximate outlines of the account to
be given of traditional topics of practical reason. For instance, essentially
occurring propositions may be said to denote an end, and if a means to that end
has been adopted, the proposition(s) specifying that means will occur, but not
essentially, in the specification of the appetitive.

But questions about the internal structure of appetitives arise because they
and the actions arising from them may be criticised and called into question in

various ways. This impetus to the analysis of appetitives is at its most powerful where an appetitive is itself subject to another appetitive—where there are wants about wants. This case acquires a special importance for value theory, and we shall revert to it in section 7.

However, the relegation of the means/end chain to the interior of an object of desire leaves another traditional problem unsolved, or rather raises it even more acutely: the problem of ακρασία, of the weakness of the will. For the position advanced here, even more sharply than a number of other positions similar in this respect, would make the means/end chain unbreakable: more precisely, our position seems to entail that if a person has a desire, and the circumstances are propitious to his action, and there are no conflicting desires, then he must act on it. Or if he does not, he cannot properly be said to have the desire.

In fact, exploration of the variety of cases to which the term 'weakness of the will' may be applied should show that this position is not paradoxical. The term is commonly applied, for instance, to cases of conflicting desires, especially when the prevailing desire is 'less worthy' or concerned with short-term goals. It may also be applied where a professed desire turns out not to be really serious: it is not a want but a wish, in our terminology. And thirdly, what is to prevent what might be called the spontaneous degeneration of a desire: what is to prevent a tendency to action simply ceasing to be? A weak-willed person in this sense would be one in whom tendencies to action did not sustain themselves very long in the absence of occasions for acting, and tended as it were to peter out even when the occasion presented itself.

It is not our present task, as we have already declared, to engage in psychological case studies. The topics of the present section, though interesting and important, belong to a more substantial treatment of psychological topics than is possible here. For it is time to make the move from what we desire to what we value.

6 Values

But how can this be done? How do we move from what is wanted to what is good? From the concrete modalities of what we called the idea of pure will, to the concrete modalities of what we called the idea of pure value?

Recall once more the model universe which was sketched in section I. Values were said to emerge in that universe at the point where we were obliged to recognise that the one and only will which *ex hypothesi* existed in it might be frustrated. The universe, we said, was 'good' so far as it conformed itself to that will, and 'bad' so far as it did not. More precisely, we suppose that the will is tending to bring about a certain state of affairs. This state of affairs could be described in some set of propositions forming a kind of blue-print for a possible future. When the universe comes to match this blue-print, that is good; when it fails to, that is bad.

Now all appetitives satisfy the propositional criterion. In their case, that is, some set of propositions (some blue-print) is always to be found which denotes the object of the appetitive. For this object we may introduce the technical term *appetitum*. The transition to values is then simple to the point of banality. For we simply state that any appetitum is a value, against which the world is to be measured, and in accordance with which it is to be transformed.

It is in this sense that I am claiming that everything that a person wants, wishes for or takes pleasure in is thereby and to that extent good. The consequences of this claim, and objections to it, will be considered in the sections that follow.

(viii) Sciences of Value

Ferdinand de Saussure wrote: 'In linguistics as in political economy we are confronted with the notion of value; *both sciences are concerned with a* system for equating things of different orders—*labour and wages in one, and a signified and a signifier in the other' (1959, I.iii.1, p. 79). These are words which should draw our attention to the extreme narrowness of philosophies of value which ignore economics and linguistics. Indeed, de Saussure found it natural to discuss value ('valeur') without referring to what we call moral values at all:*

'Even outside language all values are apparently governed by the same paradoxical principle: they are always composed:
(1) of a dissimilar *thing that can be* exchanged
for the thing of which the value is to be determined;
and
(2) of similar things that can be compared *with the thing of which the value is to be determined.*
Both factors are necessary for the existence of a value. To determine what a five-franc piece is worth one must therefore know: (1) that it can be exchanged for a fixed quantity of a different thing, e.g. bread; and (2) that it can be compared with a similar value of the same system, e.g. a one-franc piece, or with coins of another system (a dollar etc.). In the same way a word can be exchanged for something dissimilar, an idea; besides, it can be compared with something of the same nature, another word. Its value is therefore not fixed so long as one simply states that it can be 'exchanged' for a given concept, i.e. that it has this or that signification: one must also compare it with similar values, with other words that stand in opposition to it. Its content is really fixed only by the concurrence of everything that exists outside it. Being part of a system, it is endowed not only with a signification, but also and especially with a value, and this is quite different' (ib. II.iv. 2 pp. 114—5).

De Saussure's reference to exchange in his first criterion for values suggests the possibility of passing in both directions: that is, it seems that either of the two items may be taken as the value, and the other as the valued.

For instance, if the value is an amount of money (a value possessed by a coin), it may be treated as the measure of a certain quantity of labour; alternatively, that amount of labour may be treated as a value to measure that amount of money. In the case of language too, if the value is a Fregean sense (a value possessed by a word) it may be treated as the measure of a given object (as understanding the sense of the word on the shopping list enables us to judge that the object in the shopping bag is wrong), or vice versa (as recognition of the object in the bag enables us to judge whether or not a certain word is the correct word for it).

But are we not inclined to give one of the two orders priority in each system? For labour can exist without money, and objects without words. Money and language are like rulers brought in from outside to be laid against a preexisting reality. Yet this is a naive and misleading picture. Consider the case of the ruler. It may seem that things in reality are already related in terms of lengths and distances, and that a ruler brought in to measure these quantities will change nothing. Then we shall say that the value is or is possessed by this yardstick (that by whose means we measure) and that the reality which it will measure is prior to it. Yet, short of a transcendent yardstick, we must recognise that the yardstick itself is just another object. If reality already contains relations of length and so forth, then reality already contains rulers (as many as you like!). Alternatively, if reality contains no rulers, the making of something into a ruler brings into being both orders—that is, the measure and the measured. In this sense, it would be misleading to ask whether money precedes labour, or labour money, whether language precedes reality, or reality language: neither order can be understood except as forming part of a (linguistic or economic) system.

Yet is it not absurd to suggest—as we seem to have done—that things did not exist before words? Certainly; but what is not absurd is the view that things considered as having their place, and at certain points their essential place, in a certain system of multiple and possibly constitutive relations between things—things considered in some such specific way must be considered as one order in a system of which the other order is furnished by a particular language and culture. Of course, questions about the genesis, change and decay of linguistic or economic systems are in order: they are important questions. But they should not be perverted into unanswerable perplexities about the alleged priority of one order over another within the system. That way lie sterile disputes such as those between forms of materialism and idealism (do words create things, or vice versa?), or between monetarists and the apostles of productivity (is what counts in an economy the amount of work done or the amount of money in circulation—gold or productivity?).

Thus we must distinguish (which is not to say dissociate) questions about the origins of systems from questions about the operation of systems: in de Saussure's terms, we must distinguish their diachronic and synchronic aspects.

In the case of appetitive value systems in particular, we must distinguish synchronic from diachronic considerations. It will be argued in section 11 below that failure to do so is partly responsible for misconceptions about the autonomy of moral values.

There are further lessons which we may draw from de Saussure's remarks about values. The world of appetitive values must be envisaged as comprising two structured orders: first, the system of values of an individual or group which has its own internal structure or 'syntax' (and we must avoid the atomistic error of considering such systems as mere agglomerations—see section 9); and secondly, the order of the sets of states of affairs taken as able to be affected by the action of that individual or group, or as constituting its field of action; the matching of these two orders may take place in both directions within the system as a whole: we may measure the world by our values, or try to transform it in accordance with them. A further lesson is that appetitive values may be regarded as forming a segment of the totality of human value systems in the Saussurean sense—of the diverse forms of exchange and equivalence practised in and constitutive of human societies, from their language to their kinship systems and their economy: areas now the object of various sciences of value. Moral philosophy should take its place in this configuration, as a branch of the study of appetitive values.

But what is the relation between appetitive value systems and others? For instance, appetitive values clearly enter into economic, kinship and linguistic relations: it is vital to all these that we want to buy or earn something or to produce it, that men want to acquire or give a wife, that they want to say or learn something. All these wants use and bring into play and are made possible by the other value systems. They do not, however, constitute them. Relative to these desires, the other value systems become an objective framework for what is attempted.

However, this is perhaps only so at the individual level. At the communal level, these other value systems may be seen as themselves special varieties of appetitive, as expressions of the 'will' of the community, which is other than the summation of the individual wills of its members. If this were the correct view, the value systems with which we are primarily concerned would be generated by just one kind of appetitive—that involving individual desire (being the main preoccupation of the main traditions of Western moral philosophy). It is not as evident as Dummett has recently suggested (1973, p. xv) that 'moral philosophy' is prior to 'political philosophy'—though we entirely accept his claim that philosophical psychology is prior to ethics. The question here is whether individual 'psychology' is prior to group 'psychology'.

It may be held that the notion of the will which we have been using cannot admit the will of collectivities in other than an aggregative or metaphorical sense. But mere aggregation of individual wills does not allow us to deal with economic or linguistic systems, which are essentially communal. And the priority of individual willing which would be implied by taking collective willing as only paronymously so-called seems to leave no room for the essential role of society in man's emergence from an animal state, or indeed its likely role at some much earlier evolutionary stage. There is a dilemma here: we admit a collective will, and then Hegel is with us; or we give priority to the individual will, and then we have the intellectual phenomenon known in some circles as 'bourgeois individualism' in its various political and philosophical manifestations.

Let us then try to clarify the notion of the will by returning to the will of the model universe of section 1. On what grounds can that will—the source of change—hypothesised as being in that universe be said really to be in it, as opposed to acting upon it from the outside? We may try to answer this question by adding a further requirement to the model: that if the will is to be considered as forming part of the model universe (rather than being a transcendent source of change), then it must be able not only to act on the universe, but also itself to be acted on. Now if it is acted on, some change must be produced in it. But a change in it will also ex hypothesi be a change in the universe. Thus we now have a further classification of the changes which may occur in our model universe: changes which occur 'in the will' and changes which occur 'elsewhere'. We must then postulate a 'zone' in the universe which will be the zone of the will (let the quotation marks indicate that this is not necessarily a spatial zone). Now this zone will be one from which changes occurring elsewhere may originate, and which is itself liable to undergo changes originating from elsewhere. If we consider changes said to originate from it, in what does their originating from it consist? An arbitrary assignation is insufficient. At least the following two elements seem to be required: a prefiguring of the change to be produced, this prefiguring being itself a change in the zone of the will (we may call it the appetitum), and a feedback by which the change can be monitored, and if necessary correcting action taken either to adjust the change or to adjust the appetitum according to which the change is being produced. We now have the following scheme: the occurrence of an unattributable change in the zone of the will (the appetitum); the occurrence of a change outside that zone and attributable to the first; and the occurrence of further changes in the zone of the will attributable to the change produced outside, together with possible adaptations consequent upon this feedback. Of course, there are still many dark areas in this model, when we have it in mind to understand agency as we experience it and to assess philosophical views about agency as we know them. For instance, in a sense the model still fails to capture agency. It is merely stipulated that one change may produce another. Moreover, it may seem that the transcendence of the will which it was part of the purpose of this extension of the model to dispel has persisted. For why is this zone called the 'zone of the will'? Is the will still to be regarded as being outside the universe, but, as it were, attached to this special zone through some pineal gland? Or could we simply identify that zone with the will?

It is striking that the development of our model is leading us on the one hand to questions of transcendent metaphysics, and on the other to the abstract description of self-regulating organisms—to that branch of general systems theory which deals with open systems, for example. These topics will recur in section 13.

But for the present let us turn from these questions and ask what the extension of our model universe offers with respect to the question of the 'will' of collectivities. The essential step in filling out the will of the model has been to give it an 'appetitum', something which governs, and may itself be adapted by external changes. If we have good reason to attribute the existence of some such appetitum to a collectivity, then we shall have good reason to speak of the will of collectivities. There is some reason to think that languages and economic systems (for example) are entities of this kind. They belong essentially to collectivities; they cannot be explained as the aggregation of individual desires (the dependence being rather the reverse), they regulate—and are subject to adaptation as a result of the consequences of such regulation. To make the point as modestly as possible, we may say that nothing in the model yet excludes a communal will. We shall return to the form which such a will may take in section 8 below.

7 The Differentiation of Values

Moral philosophies which give pride of place to psychology by taking benevolence, pleasure, the will to power or some other psychological notion as cardinal have usually suffered from the crudeness of their psychology. Thus the simple occurrence of a certain psychological state has not in the end seemed sufficient to account for the intricacy, subtlety and variety of evaluation as we live and experience it, still less for specifically moral evaluation, whose particular qualities have led many philosophers to regard it as completely *sui generis*. And those who have held the contrary have often been forced into a kind of positivistic iconoclasm. It is important to observe that a more carefully laid basis in theoretical psychology will eliminate this weakness in such positions.

In this section, we shall outline six chief distinctions between kinds of values which flow from the analysis of appetitives so far offered and which will establish the flexibility and power of the proposed account of values.

§ 1. First, we may distinguish *primary, secondary* and *tertiary values*, according to whether the corresponding appetitive is conative, optative or fruïtive. In addition, primary and tertiary values may also occur in the *animal* and *energetic* dimensions indicated in annex (vi).

This gives an initial framework for the place of efforts, dreams and pleasures in evaluation. What a person values is given in all these modes. Primarily, however, his values are displayed and exercised in his active engagement in the world. Only subordinately do they find expression in his wishes and pleasures.

Thus if a person is a pacifist and has a tendency to act in the matter, for instance by refusing to bear arms, that there be peace is a primary value of his. But if he merely wishes for it, believing there to be no action open to him, or merely takes pleasure in it once achieved, it

49

remains a value of his but only what I call a secondary or tertiary value.

It is important to notice here that the position argued in this book is not hedonistic, either in psychology or in value theory. For it is not true in fact (still less analytically true) that human actions are always aimed at a pleasure. They are aimed simply at the fulfilment of their corresponding appetitum. Correspondingly, pleasure is not the one touchstone of value. For pleasure is not to be defined simply in terms of the satisfaction of a preexisting desire. One case of what we call disappointment is sufficient to undermine this view. Rather, as has been explained, pleasure is itself at least in many central cases a new 'desire' awakened by the very situation for which it would be a desire. Pleasure in this sense does play an important but secondary role in evaluation—just because of its appetitive structure.

§2. Secondly, there is a distinction between *quasi-values* and *real values*. A value is a quasi-value when someone acts as though it were a value of his when it is not. For instance, consider the man whose hatred of war is entirely confined to the fact that war involves injury and death for men. He does not dislike fighting as such: indeed, he may favour all forms of conflict and competition from boxing to economic struggle, but have a 'humanitarian' distaste for overt and physical suffering. This man's view will be different from that of the man who really wants peace. The state of affairs aimed at by the one is that men should not fight each other; but by the other, that men should not fight each other *and* thereby cause injury and death, where the first of these propositions does not occur essentially. Now in many situations, these men may act alike; indeed, their appetita overlap. These are the situations in which it is appropriate to say of the second man that he acts *as though* he simply wants men not to fight each other. This second appetitum—the value of peace—is a quasi-value of his.

Other cases of quasi-values occur in hypocrisy. A man acts as though he wants to give a donation to a charity, when in fact his appetitum is that he should give an offering *and* be seen to do so. Again, an apologising child acts as though he is sorry for hurting his sister by hitting her, when in fact he wants not to excuse himself, but to avoid punishment by being seen to excuse himself.

Now quasi-values are a degenerate species logically as well as evaluatively. For there is no limit to the number of quasi-values generable from any one real value by addition or subtraction of propositions. In other words the criteria of identity for quasi-values seem even more problematic than those for values themselves.

The potentially disorderly quality of quasi-values, however, is kept in check by the purposes of referring to them. If one has in mind some real value that a person could have, and that some other people do have or have had, it may be important to notice that the person already has it as a quasi-value, or to create circumstances in which he is likely to acquire such a quasi-value. One central case, for instance, is educational. In moral education, transformation of a quasi-value into a real value is a characteristic process. The parent (let us say) is concerned that his child should value truthfulness. He begins by concentrating upon it as a quasi-value, that is, by applying punishment and reward. The child at first comes to aim at the cultivation of truthfulness with a view to avoiding punishment and pleasing his parents. In due course, he may come to aim at truthfulness without qualification.

Again, when we pay attention to values which are shared in a community, the notion of quasi-values enables us to take full account of the realities of moral consensus, that it is not universally whole-hearted and single-minded. Many individuals in a community, apart from children, may tend to adhere to a given common value for extraneous reasons—may hold it as a quasi-value. This does not prevent the consensus from being real, since the appetita of the members of the community do in fact overlap at the relevant point. Nor is this a weakness in the values of the community, except from the point of view of the more stern or fanatical moral conservative. It is rather a mark of adaptability. A classical case is Mosaic law, and the challenge of Jesus to attitudes towards that law. There was, no doubt, a moral consensus in Judaic society at that time—that the law should be obeyed. No doubt some wanted to obey it and thereby avoid social disapproval, some—to obey it and avoid punishment, some—to obey it and thereby obey God, some—simply to follow the law. All these appetita overlap, so that following the law is at least a quasi-value for all the kinds of people mentioned. Thus the original Christian value—to love God and your neighbour, and therefore among other things follow the law (in which arguably following the law does not occur essentially), though revolutionary from many points of view, nevertheless had important continuities with the past, retaining following the law as a quasi-value.

Thus, quasi-values, too easily despised in the individual for hypocrisy, provide in the community a great means of conserving the moral experience of the past, and a fertile ground for moral evolution or even revolution.

§3. A third distinction to be drawn is that between *open* and *closed* values. A closed value is a value such that there could be a time by which the corresponding desire could have been fulfilled—for instance, that John should not quarrel with Roland over their inheritance. An open value is a value such that there could not be a time by which the desire could have been fulfilled—for instance, that mankind should live in peace. For even if universal peace were established in the year 2000 (which would conform to the value), war might break out again in 2001; thus that there should be peace is an open value, never to be definitively fulfilled. John and Roland, however, cannot quarrel over their inheritance after one of them dies, so that if they have not quarrelled over it before this time, the desire that they should not do so (whoever may have had it) will have been definitively fulfilled, and thus the value corresponding to it is a closed value.

(ix) Eschatologies

It may seem that this distinction between open and closed values breaks down in face of any eschatological moral position. For the last day is precisely the time at which so-called open values are found to be fulfilled or not.

Yet the last day is a very special sort of 'time'—a final or limiting time. In religious eschatologies, paradise is outside or beyond time as we know it. In Marxist eschatology, the final utopia is equally beyond time as we know it (that is, time as determined by the strictly historical process of class struggle, warring and resolved contradiction, etc.).

Thus we may either deny that the last day is a time, or say that it is that limiting time at which even open values become closed. For closed values are already closed within the temporal sphere; but open values are closed only sub specie aeternitatis.

7 The Differentiation of Values

§ 4. A fourth distinction to be made is between *negative* and *positive* values. A negative value occurs where the proposition(s) occurring essentially in the corresponding appetitum is (are) negative. A value that is not negative is positive.

This is a logically trivial distinction, since we could always pass from a negative proposition (say, one in the semantics of which must occur an expression of the form $\sim F(a)$) to a positive (in which $G(a)$ takes the place of $\sim F(a)$), merely by defining G as the contradictory of F (so that (x) $(Fx \equiv \sim Gx)$).

Moreover, equivalences of this kind certainly occur in natural languages. Are we to say, for instance, that my desire that you should be present is positive, while my desire that you should *not* be absent is negative?

The answer is that while there are appetitives which may indifferently have either positive or negative form, such as the one just mentioned, nevertheless, such conversions are not generally possible. Let us consider moralities characterised by prohibitions: if these prohibitions could indifferently be transformed into exhortations, our description of these moralities as concerned above all to forbid or stop certain actions would be a purely formal or artificial one. We do not feel it to be so: 'Do not kill' seems unequivocally to be a prohibition (even if transformed into a superficially unnegated form such as: 'Leave alive'); likewise, 'Do not commit adultery' (even if transformed into 'Be sexually faithful to your spouse'). It is not our present purpose to discuss what could justify our persuasion of the priority of the negative form in these cases (the issue is related to that raised by Nelson Goodman's 'grue' emeralds, and Hempel's 'non-black non-ravens', as Quine's discussion of the natural or animal priority of certain predicates in his essay 'Natural Kinds' clearly shows): it is enough to notice that it is such a persuasion which ensures that the statement of any corresponding appetita will be in negative form, so that the criterion mentioned above may be applied in distinguishing negative from positive values. The pattern for this distinction in the model universe of section 1 and annex (viii) will be that between cases in which the will has to bring about a change in order to fulfil its appetitum and cases in which it has to abstain from bringing about, or resist a change.

§ 5. Fifthly, there is a distinction between first order values, and values of higher orders. A first order value is a value in the specification of which no other values occur essentially; a second order value is one in whose specification one or more first-order values occur essentially; a third order value, one in whose specification one or more second order values occur essentially, and so on. Put simply, this means that higher order values occur when there are wants about wants; when, in describing the state of affairs which is a man's appetitum in some case, we have to include reference to other appetita or wants, whether of the man himself, or of others. Take the case of a man wanting peace; we may find that what he really wants is that people should not *want* to harm each other, while another man might merely be concerned that any such harm be prevented.

But what of the non-essential occurrence of a value in the specification of another? A man wants to marry a certain girl. The marriage is unlikely to take place unless the girl also wants to marry him. Knowing this, the man will have the following appetitum (to give it in some more detail): that the girl should want to marry him, and that the marriage should take place. But there are two possible cases here: one in which he really does want the girl to want to marry him, because the kind of relationship with her which he envisages would be impossible without that desire on her part, and another, let us say, in which he wants the marriage for purely economic reasons, so that, though he wants the girl's consent, it is—as we say—only as a means, and if the marriage were to take place without such a desire on her part, his desire would be satisfied. The reference to the girl's desire, therefore, does not occur essentially in the specification of his desire (in the second case), since his desire could be satisfied by a state of affairs in which she did not have the desire to marry him.

To take another example, suppose that a man makes a private sacrifice to help someone in need. He doesn't do it from a Kantian sense of duty—he merely wants to help. In his case, we are dealing with a first order value. If we praise his action, we introduce a new value—our own: for we want people to have such desires, including ourselves.

We may illustrate the point further with yet another and more complicated example. A boy is progressing well at school, but unsatisfied. He is bored, inarticulate and withdrawn. He seems to want a change, without knowing what. The boy's parents, noting what they take to be his desire for revolt, send him to another school where they hope that this desire will be suitably satisfied. Here is a second order value. Now the promoters of this school want to satisfy the desires of parents to satisfy their children's desires for revolt. This is a third order value. In a letter to a newspaper, a traditionally minded correspondent expresses his hostility to such schools, saying essentially that he does not want the state of affairs in which the promoters of schools want the state of affairs in which the parents want the state of affairs in which the teachers want the state of affairs in which the child who wants revolt should have his desire satisfied. This is a fifth order value (though style, as well as other considerations, may well have obscured this hierarchical appetitive structure).

Is there any limit to this ladder of values? There is, I think, no limit of principle, save that there are desires the specification of which essentially includes reference to other desires *regardless of their order*. For instance, I may want the good of others to take precedence over all my other desires. Now this desire, though it may conflict both logically and practically with other desires which I have or may have, as well as with other desires of other persons, yet includes all my other desires within its scope, and subordinates them explicitly to one goal, whatever their order may be. A value of this kind may be called an *architectonic value*, after Aristotle. There could not be a value of higher order, though there could of course be other architectonic values (even in the same person) in conflict with it.

Here, then, is a central complication that we meet in moving from the model universe of section 1 to the world of our experience, that wants come into conflict, not only with practical intransigencies, but also with each other, even in one person; it is this fact which introduces higher order values into our world, for it is so that our desires come to be directed not only upon certain states of the universe, but also upon bringing about or eliminating desires for those states. And it is in this region that much moral activity takes place, that we are urged to love each other, to cultivate inner virtues, that we are praised, blamed, punished and rewarded. To this extent, Kant was right in fastening on the motive of duty as a locus of

morality. This is so, however, only because of the specific imperfec-
tion of our world which is the disharmony, including the inner
disharmony of human desires. If this disharmony did not exist, most
higher order values, and with them duty, would be superfluous and
would disappear. So too, we might argue, specifically moral values
would disappear, being that refraction in values which is produced by
their intersection with the impurities of the world we experience.

§6. There is a further, and particularly notable distinction between
what I shall call *relative* and *absolute* values. A value is relative if
reference to the person whose value it is occurs essentially in the
specification of the value; and a value is absolute if it is not relative.
This is a distinction related to the notions of selfishness and altruism. It
may be clarified by an example. Suppose that there is a man in danger
of drowning in a lake. A bystander notices his predicament, and
wants him to be saved. So he prepares to dive in, but as he is about to
do so, a boat comes into view, and the man is rescued by someone in
the boat. Now suppose that the bystander's original desire was
this—that he should swim to the drowing man and save him. Did
mention of the bystander (as the rescuer) occur essentially in the
description of the object of his desire? If his desire would be satisfied
by a rescue from the boat, then mention of him does not occur
essentially: what he really wanted was that someone should rescue the
man, believing at first that he would himself have to be that person. In
the other case, his desire would be frustrated by the boat coming to
the rescue. His desire might essentially have included this—that *he*
should be the rescuer. Then reference to him will have occurred
essentially in the specification of the value. It would then be a case of a
relative value; whereas the other situation, where he simply wants the
man to be rescued (no matter by whom), would be an absolute value.

Thus on our basis in theoretical psychology, we are able to create
an array of independently varying distinctions in values. Every value
must be situable for each of the six distinctions, but no position on any
one distinction requires any position on any other. Our account may
be reviewed schematically as shown in the diagram on the next page.
This diagram illustrates succinctly the flexibility of the proposed
account of values. It is a flexibility that is dramatically increased when
we recognize that we have largely restricted ourselves to single
values. In fact, as has been briefly noticed, some evaluative attitudes,
even in a single person, may be appetitively complex. A particular

Appetitivity	Sincerity	Scope	Positivity	Relativity	Order
primary	real	open	positive	absolute	first
					second
secondary					third
tertiary	quasi	closed	negative	relative	. . . . .
					architectonic

case of admiration, for example, might involve first—wanting the admired person to be imitated in respect of his desires (a primary, real, open, positive, absolute, second-order value), acting as though one wished to be the other person (a secondary, quasi, closed, positive, relative, first-order value), as well as taking pleasure in his existence (a tertiary, real, closed, positive, absolute, first-order value).

But what of specifically moral values? Before we consider them, we must progress from the analysis of particular wills and particular values to some account of multiplicities of wills and multiplicities of values.

8 Wills in Harmony and Wills in Concert

Until now we have been primarily concerned with an account of value and desire based on the model universe with one will of section 1. But the world we know has a multitude of wills. Thus for any given value we have three possibilities: first, it may be a value of only one person (an appetitum of only one will); secondly, it may be a value shared by a number of persons (where several wills are directed at the same appetitum—wills in harmony); third, it may be a group value (where the appetitum is such as to be possessed only by a group of wills—wills in concert).

The difference between the second and the third cases becomes manifest in the distinction between actions that may be performed by individuals severally, and actions that may be performed only by collectivities. For instance, rioting, discussing, making war, electing, going on strike are all actions properly or primarily performed by a group. Correspondingly, the desire or tendency to perform them exists in the group, and the corresponding value is essentially collective. These group values are different from values shared by a group, where the members of the group severally desire the same object, like the punters, trainers, jockey and owner all wanting the same horse to win.

It will be convenient to speak of those whose appetita constitute a given value as the 'reference group'. We may now elaborate the earlier point. A reference group always has at least one member. In the case of some values it may necessarily have more than one member. Moreover, a reference group having more than one member or may not be identifiable independently of the correspond-ing appetitum; that is, the persons concerned may or may not have something which brings them together beyond the sharing of this value. For instance, the desire that Pegasus should win the three-thirty is likely to be the only thing that marks off its reference group; whereas war can be made only by a nation, so that the group that makes war must also be identifiable as the nation that it is (the term 'nation' here should be allowed to cover various marginal cases). In such a case, of course, the fact that war is the somehow determined will of the nation does not imply that it is the will of every member of that group.

However, the distinction between wills in harmony and wills in concert, though it may seem clear when we refer to some chosen examples, gives rise to perplexity. For the case of wills 'in concert' has in fact been explained by reference to *a concerted will*: the question then arises—what in these cases is the relation between the wills that are in concert and the concerted will? What is the will of the collectivity in rioting, and what is its relation to the wills of the individual rioters? What is the concerted will in discussing, and what its relation to the wills of the parties to the discussion? and so forth.

Let us start by considering the case of a discussion. Could we not understand this activity by reference to the wills of the (say two) parties to the discussion without in addition appealing to a concerted will? We may grant that discussing can be regarded as an action performed by a collectivity, but deny that it is anything over and above the contributive actions of those who take part in the discussion. In other words, a discussion is nothing other than a sequence of speeches in the question/answer relation, or some other such relation, and the successive utterance of such speeches with the appropriate intentions constitutes a discussion. We have no need of a collective will.

Consider the following minimal discussion:

'What is the number of the house?'
'Seventeen.'

This, it seems, can be simply accounted for as follows. John is concerned with some house, but he does not know its number. Consequently, he asks Richard, whom he thinks possibly to know the number, and in asking the question he is trying to get Richard to tell him it. Richard, on the other hand, in replying (we assume that he is not lying or answering at random), is trying to inform John of the number of that house. Schematically, John's aim is that John should know the number, and he tries to bring it about that Richard should try to bring it about that John should know the number.

It may seem very clear that two wills are enough here, that we do not need a third will—that of the John–Richard collectivity. In other words, if 'John knows p' be represented by '$K_j p$', and 'Richard brings it about that p' by '$D_r p$', then the conversation above can be sufficiently represented by the formula $D_j D_r K_j p$.

But there is a weakness here. It is true that if we take the conversation as given, the above representation is adequate. We take it that $D_a p$ implies p. Then from $D_j D_r K_j p$ we can infer $D_r K_j p$, which is true of the conversation, and from that in turn $K_j p$, which is also true at the end of the conversation. But by starting from the conversation as a whole, we are begging the question, which is whether that whole can be treated by summing the wills of John and Richard. For what is John's action, considered as *one of the two* constituent actions of this discussion? It is that he asks a question—and asking a question is not bringing it about that an interlocutor causes you to know the answer; it is trying to bring that about. Equally, Richard's reply is not of itself a bringing it about that John knows the number, it is an attempt to bring that about. Then what brings it about that the first attempt (the question) can achieve its goal (and consequently the second also)? It seems to be a tacit agreement of Richard and John that they should engage in a question–answer exchange such that if successful it would conform to the pattern schematically given above. This specific agreement is of course itself made possible by more general conventions of language and society. What is suggested, then, is that to understand a discussion as an interaction of two wills, we have to appeal to a joint will that the discussion should proceed according to a certain pattern. Of course, this joint will need not be exercised in any other way than in the several actions which constitute the discussion. It is that which plays the same role with respect to the components of the discussion as rules of inference play with respect to the steps of an argument. Thus, though we need to refer to the collective will, we must not treat it as another coordinate component of the discussion. Attempting to do this would produce something of the form $D_{j-r} D_j D_r K_j p$, and would be subject to the analogue of Lewis Carroll's Achilles and the Tortoise paradox.

Let us consider an example of the conditions which must be jointly secured in order that the discussions proceed. John and Richard must assure that they are speaking about the same house. But then why should this assurance be regarded as something achieved by the collectivity of John and Richard? Let us allow p to be the proposition ' "The house" in the discussion is the one and only house such that . . .;' then the condition to be secured is that both John and Richard know this—$K_j p \,\&\, K_r p$. But can this not be brought about by, say, John? We should then have an expression of the form $D_j (K_j p \,\&\, K_r p)$. But there is a flaw here. John may know that he will use the term 'the house' in the required way in the discussion (he may intend to do so), but he cannot know that it will be so used in the discussion unless he also knows that Richard will so use it. But the only reason he could have for supposing that Richard will so use it, *ex hypothesi*, is that Richard will follow his stipulation. But this is viciously circular, since $D_j (K_j p \ \& \ K_r p)$ was introduced precisely as giving the form of that stipulation. Here then is a specific example of the need to refer to a superordinate (joint) will, and of the importance of not treating it as coordinate with the individual wills.

It is indeed an example of the role of conventions in language and understanding, of that 'common world of the understanding' which we had occasion to discuss in annex (iii). In outline, just as language and understanding in general require reference to communal arrangements and their maintenance, to some kind of communal will: so too in a particular linguistic situation, the participants must as a collectivity be taken to see to it that the specific conditions obtain which are necessary for the success of their particular project.

But suppose that both John and Richard as a matter of fact do make the required assumptions: why do we need additional reference to the pair as a collectivity? It is because the assumptions required can only be specified as those which are to govern *their* discussion: but the discussion only exists if the assumptions are made. Just as we have seen a connection on the one hand between the problem we are discussing and the Lewis Carroll paradox, so on the other we see a connection with traditional social contract paradoxes, by which there could not be a first contract since any contract implies a prior contract in terms of which it may be established.

On this side, we may profitably recall Russell Grice's position in his *The Grounds of Moral Judgement*, or that of Rawls in *A Theory of Justice*. The contract becomes in a special way hypothetical: we draw attention to situations in which it would be in the interest of the parties to them to have contracted or to contract to act in a certain way. The analogy in our case will be that the parties to the discussion should áct as though they had agreed that they should jointly ensure its conformity to certain conditions. This requirement of conformity is sometimes realised in the person of a chairman, who is supposed to be not a party to the discussion coordinate with the others, but a superordinate representative and guardian of what makes the discussion possible.

An account now takes shape of certain actions of collectivities. Beyond the several constituent actions of the members of the collectivity, appeal is made *in addition* to the will of the collectivity as such, since the conventions or contract underlying the collective action can be explained only by such an appeal. But we must beware of an unbalanced diet of examples. This account of the *concerted will* is being constructed on the basis of a solitary example, that of the highly sophisticated collective action of discussing. Moreover, discussing is a dubious candidate for a collective action. And though it is instructive to have discovered a need in this marginal case to appeal to the collectivity as well as to its members, we cannot be confident that the account emerging will apply to more central cases.

For instance, we have mentioned rioting as a case of collective action. We shall not debate the *centrality* of this example. It is in any case clear that the rioters are not bound together by any convention or contract, even implicit or hypothetical. There could not be a chairman of a riot, whose task it would be to see that the parties to the riot broadly observed some agreed procedure.

But it might be maintained that a riot could be 'stage-managed': it is a mere turn of idiom that this stage-manager would not be called a chairman. But no: there is at least an implicit chairman in every discussion; for the chairman's role is part of the structure of discussion as such—the chairman stands for the collectivity, and the collectivity stands by certain conventions, and the discussion stands on those conventions. But the stage-manager of a riot would not be structurally part of it. It is not only that a riot could take place without being stage-managed: but the stage-manager of a riot that was stage-managed would be outside it, calculating the effect of various interventions on the mob which was under his observation. The chairman is on the platform with the speakers; the chairman may be up-stage: but the stage-manager is off-stage.

In the one collectivity, then, there is a strongly articulated internal structure assigning various roles to its individual members in various circumstances: indeed, the collectivity has its existence in and by maintaining this structure. In the other, however, we find a virtual absence of such structure: the individual who riots in a way ceases to be an individual—he 'loses himself', he is 'swept along', he becomes 'just one of the mob', he is 'carried away'. The rioter does not of course cease to be an individual organism: he breathes and moves; but he is more likely to run than walk; much more likely to shout than talk; and he tends to stop thinking as an individual: such instrumental intelligence as is displayed in a riot is displayed at the collective level by actions like changing route to avoid an obstacle. But it is 'intelligence' of a very low order, and rather easily outwitted. The rioting mob is superhuman—for it is composed of individual human beings and is an entity of a higher order than they (in some sense): but it is subhuman—for the rioting individuals tend to lose human characteristics, and the resulting collective being is more bestial than human. This is perhaps why the parties to a riot as well as its victims may be frightened by it—and frightened in more than a merely prudential way.

Differences between our two examples may be further illustrated by considering ways in which collective actions of the two kinds may be balked. How might one set about sabotaging a discussion? One range of methods depends upon a crude physical interference with what makes the discussion possible: we bodily separate the parties to the discussion—we cut a telephone line—we turn on a radio so loud that the participants can no longer hear each other. But there is another range of procedures aimed with greater or less subtlety at disturbing the tacit conventions of the discussion. An unsubtle example: use of a word considered *obscene* in a *polite* discussion is likely to stop it, since there will rarely be any way of regarding it as a move in that discussion; or again, the introduction of an irrelevance into a directed or purposive discussion may have the same effect. The latter case is of some interest, since 'changing the subject' is in fact allowed for in many, if not all kinds of discussion (it is even called for: the bore, too, is a conversation stopper). In what is loosely characterised as 'casual conversation' the governing conventions are rather weak and there are few *thematic* restraints on changing the subject; there are, however, restraints on frequency (it would not do for *each* speech of a party to a two-person conversation to be a change of subject). In other cases, though there may be much stronger restraints on changing the subject, they are nevertheless not absolute: in other words, breaching these restraints does not necessarily end the discussion. For it may be treated as a tacit proposal for a change in the governing convention, and a reply may establish and further delimit that change.

Of course, it is rather rare for the establishment, observation or alteration of such conventions to be a matter for conscious attention. On the other hand, consciousness of them at a theoretical level emerged rather early in Western thought. And it emerged interestingly in two rival models of the direction of discussion and speech in awareness of such conventions, and of the possibilities of exploiting, developing or codifying them. For the proponents of the rival versions of this new insight, their dispute was of the first importance.

Nothing could be further from Plato's Academy than the school of Isocrates. But the rivalry between philosophy and rhetoric was as nothing to the layman, for whom, as Aristophanes had already made clear in his parody of Socrates, the *Clouds*, these men, whatever their rival doctrines, indifferently exploited their indecent study of conventions of speech to 'make the better argument appear worse, and the worse better'. For the Platonists, truth was independent of forms of speech, though attainable by privileged forms of argument: the rest was trickery or ornament. Here were the impulses to formal logic (and the first important step here would be taken in Aristotle's *Topics* with the codification and classification of certain underlying conventions of discussion), and to the philosophers' notion of timeless and context-free propositions. For the rhetoricians, on the other hand, the proposition is an abstract monstrosity, and the logical schemata of inference a mischievous extrapolation from the realities of human communication through language. Since this seminal dispute philosophy and literature have been increasingly at odds in Western thought. And if the rhetorician is devoted to speech, philosophy, at times, has seemed to be devoted to its annihilation: Socratic irony is the supreme conversation stopper: the mother and father of red herrings and indecent interjections.

But it is not necessary to substantiate these brief observations on the genesis of rhetoric and philosophy in order to show the possibility of disturbing or breaking off a discussion by interfering with or playing on its underlying conventions. The question that now concerns us is whether there is any parallel to such interventions in the case of another form of collective behaviour, rioting, in which we have agreed that no such conventions are present. Certainly, the analogues of cutting the telephone line, or drowning the conversation with loud noise and so on, are to be found in the armoury of a riot squad, though its weapons are more sinister. But, as we have seen, a conversation can be stopped by tampering directly with its mechanisms: can this be done for a riot? The following case was once reported to me. A rioting crowd paused at a police barrier, in a moment of tension; the man in charge of the police stepped forward, and all eyes were on him: would his action unlock the next stage of the riot? He did not harangue the crowd, raise his arms, or issue a threat—he gave no orders to the squad of police. Instead, he took a bunch of keys from his pocket and juggled with them: the riot ended.

Now the creation of a mob from a group of individuals seems to require, as we have seen, a certain loss of or merging of their individual identity. The mob once constituted has a limited number of rather simple responses to a few broadly defined categories of situation, such as situations which present obvious obstacles to its objective, and situations which offer an obvious approach to that objective. In the case quoted, the whole attention of the mob came to be directed upon an unassimilable action: the juggling resisted interpretation as a threat or as an encouragement. Thus, in attending to this event, the mob ceased to exist, dissolving into an aggregate of individual people in the same place all observing a particular inconsequential act.

Now if we may disrupt a discussion by tampering with its *conventions*, what would we be tampering with in such methods of disrupting a riot? Here we seem to need a theory of sympathy, a theory by which it would be possible to explain forms of solidarity between men not based even on implicit conventions.

A serious study of sympathy belongs to various sciences, and we cannot embark upon it here. But the general form of the questions to be asked about collective action in collectivities based on sympathy, as in collectivities based on convention, is: how are such superordinate persons constructed? This is no more or less than the question how human society, organisationally or affectively, is constituted. As I have said, it is not part of our task here even to sketch the emergence of organisations, of possibilities of mass action, of corporate personalities, or to outline the diversity of types of communal will from that exercised by a highly organised and hierarchical bureaucracy, to that evident in a casual street-corner conversation, or manifest in the pure violence of an undifferentiated rioting mob.

But when we consider these phenomena, our individualistic predilections may make us revert obstinately to the question which has recurred in various forms throughout this section: are not individual wills prior to collective wills? Do not the latter exist only upon the condition that individuals freely and for as long or as brief a period as they wish enter into their creation? A rioter may at any moment walk away; an interlocutor may at any moment leave or sabotage the discussion, and so on. These observations, no doubt, are true. But they display a distracting anxiety for individual freedom.

It is an anxiety provoked by the idea that a collective will might be a mysterious force able to subject individual wills to its determination. We should dismiss it; and remark that collectivities make individuals possible just as much as individuals make collectivities possible. It is a mistake to think of either form of the will either as prior or indeed as firmly delimited. This is what gives importance to the notion of wills in concert: for it is only in special cases that the will of a collectivity (the concerted will) can be thought of as having an existence of its own (through legal fictions, and so on); and equally only for special purposes that individual wills can be thought of as having an existence independent of collectivities (in the sphere of morality, for instance).

In our model universe, we have only one will, and we have supposed the delimitation of its 'zone' to be unproblematic. If additional wills are introduced into the model, we shall not be able to exclude the case of an overlapping of zones: at this point, an atomistic/additive account of their interaction ceases to be suitable, for we are quickly faced with analogues in theoretical psychology of the three-body problem. This is a point to which we shall return in section 13. Meanwhile it will be enough to note that we give priority neither to the individual will (in the manner of Mill) nor to the collective will (in the manner of Hegel).

9 Values in Harmony and Values in Concert

In addition to the harmony or concert of wills in respect of their values, we must consider the harmony or concert of values themselves.

In the first place, values can be regarded as forming systems by what we may call *compresence*, that is, their presence together in the same person (or independently identifiable group of persons). However, mere compresence will not sufficiently account for the unity which value systems may be experienced as having. In fact, it is a matter of experience that the value systems of individuals and groups do not spring from arbitrary collocations of appetita. What further principles then concur in defining value systems?

We may appeal to a second and a third criterion: to *compatibility* and *compracticability*. Now it is clear that it is not a condition of there being a value system that its component values should be perfectly compatible and compracticable. Indeed, the modification or collapse of value systems in the face of emergent contradictions (whether logical or practical) is a leading feature of the history of mankind, as well as a frequent dilemma for the individual man. But the very fact that these modifications and collapses occur shows that compatibility and compracticability act as a constraint upon value systems. The more blatant the incompatibilities or incompracticabilities, the less likely is a system of values to survive or even to exist. For the group or the individual will in the end be obliged to alter at least some of its values. There is a limit to good luck, and to the possibilities of self-deceit.

However, the compresence of a number of values in a person or group as constrained by their compatibility and compracticability is still, it seems, insufficient to account for that other unifying feature of value-systems which we may provisionally call their style. What constitutes such a style has been a recurrent problem for historians and social scientists, who, from Marx and Durkheim to Weber and Mannheim, have given very different answers to the question. How in general such an investigation of style is possible will be the topic of annex (x).

(x) Thematics

We return to part of the argument of annex (iii), where a justification was offered for the use of a notion of a proposition. Now at that point, a proposition was defined as what is expressed by a set of sentences where the set is granted to be the set of sentences which are for a certain purpose interchangeable. If we ask a similar question about the identity of a sentence, similar problems arise. A sentence too is to be defined with respect to a set of what have come to be called 'token sentences'. But yet again similar questions can arise about the phonetic identity of a token sentence.

There seems to be here a scheme of argument capable of repeated application, and generating a hierarchy of formal entities whose properties and relations may be investigated at each level by the appropriate enquiry: phonology, morphology, syntax, semantics.

But is there any reason for supposing that propositions are the highest entities in this ladder? That is, just as interchangeability for a set of sentences is the genesis of propositions, could there be a higher order interchangeability between a set of propositions which would be the genesis of a yet higher order entity?

Our first answer might be: certainly not. For it is necessary to language that while we may use a number of different sentences indifferently to express the same proposition, we may not propound a number of propositions indifferently; for to propound a different proposition is to say something different; and it is never indifferent that we say something different. But this, of course is to beg the question. The question is precisely whether sometimes in saying something different, we are at another level saying the same thing.

It seems that there are such cases. Consider for instance a socialist saying of someone: 'He disapproves of death duties', or 'He is unwilling to put his child in the State educational system', or 'He opposes nationalisation'. It is clear that we are dealing here with three different propositions (each of which evidently could be expressed in many different sentences). But it is also true that there could be circumstances in which the propounding of any of these propositions would amount to the same. Indeed, it is in general possible to ask what a person is trying to say, although it is quite clear what propositions he is propounding.

Thus the postulation of higher order entities bearing a similar relation to propositions to that which they bear to sentences turns out to be far from idle. I introduce the term 'thema' for a higher order entity of this kind. And now, corresponding to the study of the relation between sentences and propositions (namely, semantics), we have a study of the relation between propositions and themata, which we might call 'thematics', or 'hermeneutics'.

Of course, many objections to this picture of language, with or without its corollary of themata, can be made. In particular, it might be held that it, like much other progeny of Aristotle's De Interpretatione, *supposes erroneously that the assertoric uses of language are primary. Is the point that I have made, for instance, by speaking of the relation between propositions and themata, simply a confused version of Austin's distinction between the illocutionary and the perlocutionary act? This is a question which I shall not pursue here. I shall allow myself merely to indicate a line of answer by the assertion that the ability to propound propositions is central to all uses of language from assertion to exclamation, and that themata enter as a corollary, once the door has been opened to propositions.*

Let us look more closely at themata, and begin by considering the relation between syntactic, semantic and what we may call hermeneutic rules. An important initial point to observe is that each set of rules may be seen as constructing higher order units out of lower order elements. These units are then subject to further rules, become themselves elements out of which entities of a higher order again are constituted.

But how are all these rules related? We might at first think them to be logically independent. That is, in the case of syntax and semantics, we might think that a particular syntax imposes no particular semantics, and a particular semantics no particular syntax. But this view is subject to important qualifications. First, if a language is to be sufficiently powerful, it is essential that semantic rules should cover open classes of syntactic units, these classes, plainly, being defined and related syntactically: in this way, a given syntax will impose semantic restrictions (apparent counter-examples from codes and ciphers are properly dismissed as parasitic). Equally, though it would be possible, given a particular set of semantic rules, to substitute different syntactic units for the ones on which they presently operate, there are again restrictions on how this could be done if inconsistency in the application of semantic rules as applied to the new units is to be avoided. In general, to give a string of words a meaning is thereby to give it a syntax, to make it into a sentence. In a favourite example, giving one meaning rather than another to the string 'I like cooking apples', is also giving it one syntax rather than another, making it one sentence rather than another.

Now, like syntactic and semantic rules, semantic and hermeneutic rules are restrictedly independent. Nothing about the proposition that a man disapproves of death duties compels it to be taken as conveying the thema which it did in the context hinted at above. Yet, plainly, the proposition delimits a range of themata. Equally, nothing about the thema compels it to be conveyed by that particular proposition. But, to pursue the analogy, in taking a syntactic unit (a sentence) as conveying a certain thema, we are thereby taking it as expressing a certain proposition. For instance, in taking the syntactic unit 'He disapproves of death duties' to convey the same thema as may be taken to be conveyed by 'He opposes nationalisation', we are thereby taking that syntactic unit as expressing the proposition which is also expressed by 'He believes inheritance taxes to be wrong', rather than that which is also expressed by 'He thinks that supposed duties arising in the event of a death should be disregarded'.

Thus, the notion of higher order meanings given or perhaps hidden in lower order ones—the notion of themata—is acquiring some substance. But there are some serious challenges to it. First, does it represent an unnecessary multiplication of entities? Secondly, is it a notion which would have application only in what are broadly called the cultural sciences? Thirdly, is this corollary of a traditional view of language which we have been trying to establish actually no more than a reductio ad absurdum of that view?

First, then, ought we to use Occam's razor and deny the existence of themata altogether? It might be argued that these themata can only be set up by tacitly adopting the false view that the same sentences always or generally express the same propositions. In a certain context, let us admit, the sentences 'He disapproves of death duties', 'He is unwilling to put his child in the State educational system', and 'He opposes nationalisation' might be interchangeable. But so far from showing that we are dealing here with different propositions conveying the same thema, the case should simply be regarded as one in which the three sentences are used or understood to express the same proposition. Let us not multiply entities beyond what is needful: the work to be done by themata can in fact be done by propositions alone.

This objection is, I think, easily disposed of. It is perhaps enough merely to repeat the observation made earlier, that it is perfectly possible to wonder what a man is getting at even when it is clear what propositions he is propounding. For instance, let someone admit an error. He does so by expressing a certain proposition. And he is understood to do so by being understood to express that proposition. But in admitting his error he may further be expressing a desire for reconciliation with the person addressed. In this case, he is conveying the thema of a desire for reconciliation by expressing the proposition that he was in error; and although certainly this is not the only means by which such a desire might be conveyed, if it is so conveyed, it is indeed by the use of that proposition that the man conveys it. Again, 'He disapproves of death duties' may be true or false. But even granted that the propositional ambiguity of this sentence is resolved, and that we know the proposition to be true—a thematic ambiguity will remain.

Thus the first objection is not enough to make thematics collapse into semantics. Let us turn to the second difficulty. Does thematics exist only in the human sciences? The following argument may be put forward. Any plausible examples that may be given of themata are in the field of human behaviour and expression. It is certainly the case that human behaviour calls for interpretation multiply and at many different levels. It always makes sense to ask, given any description of a man's linguistic or non-linguistic behaviour, what he's getting at. This is a fact that raises many vexed philosophical problems concerning motives, intentions, reasons for action, and so forth, as well as many empirical questions in the same area. The human sciences try to deal with such questions, and such endeavours themselves raise conceptual problems. But such problems, which belong essentially to theoretical psychology, are simply obscured by wrapping them up in the terminology of 'themata', by suggesting that they arise as problems in the theory of meaning. It is, after all, clear that a proposition like 'The sun is about 93 million miles from the Earth', or 'The photon has no charge', does not convey any thema. What has been called a thema is really nothing more than a motive or intention with which someone acts or speaks.

This is a more substantial and difficult objection. It will be suggested in reply that the view in the theory of meaning put forward is in fact quite general, and the argument will proceed by showing how themata are after all conveyed by propositions in the natural sciences.

Let us start by considering the shop-window presentation of scientific conclusions. In such presentation, the scientist may lay out what he knows as a deductive system, with general laws at the top, and particular observation statements at the bottom. The system may be presented by the most hard-nosed as a closed system such that the topmost laws are to be understood as doing nothing more than stating more concisely what is already stated by all the bottom-most observation statements.

But given a hierarchically ordered system of the kind described, can we see there any place for themata? The answer stands out. Thematic relations between propositions will be those which are given by the grouping of those propositions under some higher proposition (or law). Thus the proposition that the photon has no charge will, together with many others, be taken to convey as a thema the corpuscular theory of light.

There is an objection to be met here. Are we not dealing with a single ordered system? Has it not been claimed that the higher order propositions which it contains state no more than is already stated by lower-order propositions? Must it not then be that there is only one set of semantic rules, and that between various propositions in the system, nothing more recondite is needed than relations of implication? Consider the analogy of a game of chess. Here the rules of the game specify how the pieces are to be moved. It is a consequence of these rules that there are other higher order rules governing sequences of positions of the whole board. In turn, from these positions, we can construct sequences of moves (including those called gambits), and there will be yet higher order rules governing these yet higher order entities. The introduction of themata in language is like the introduction of higher order entities (and rules) at chess: it is a superfluous elaboration upon the set of semantic rules, just as the other is a superfluous elaboration upon the one set of rules of chess.

This objection does not cut as deep as might seem. For though themata are indeed a superfluous construct in the case of the shop-window positivist formulation of scientific results, they are precisely not so in the case of the practice of scientific enquiry. For in that practice, the 'thematic' relations between scientific propositions are precisely a crucial problem, and moreover the thematic ambiguity of scientific propositions is a crucial means of advance in its capacity to suggest future lines of enquiry. Consider the thematic ambiguity of propositions suggesting that the atom was like a small solar system. The investigable uncertainty of how far such propositions concerning atoms could be correlated with established propositions concerning planetry systems properly so-called was a heuristic advantage.

A similar point may be made for a case already considered in annex (iv) above, that of Joule's treatment of heat as a form of energy. And we at once remark that themata have brought us to the borders of paronymy. For it is often the thematic principles characterising different domains which also suggest ways of relating or amalgamating those different domains.

Thus the case of the natural sciences, while it seemed at first to provide a strong counter-example to the claim that the notion of a thema is required in a general theory of meaning, in fact turns out to provide further exemplification of the claim.

But the claim still has to meet a third objection: that it should be taken seriously only as a reductio ad absurdum of the theory of language of which it is allegedly a corollary. On this objection we shall say that things have already gone wrong at the point at which we begin speaking even of semantic rules, as though they not only existed, but were analogous to syntactic rules. There is, it will be urged, no branch of enquiry called semantics at all—there is nothing left over for it from all the special sciences and disciplines. Still less, if semantics be banished, shall we find any home for 'thematics'. The chess *analogy might have been taken more seriously: for clearly there are no higher order rules beyond what corresponds to syntax—namely, the rules of chess.*

In reply to this objection let it be said that in fact the argument of the present section in no way requires the autonomy of semantics and thematics. Further, the elaboration of the chess analogy was a bad move by the objector: that a certain move will constitute 'putting the opponent into check' is indeed part of the semantics of chess; that another move is an 'attacking move', or that **B** *to* **K3** *made by Fischer in a match against Byrne played when he was 13 was 'one of the best in the history of chess' (Gerald Abrahams,* The Chess Mind*)—these are hermeneutic judgements, bringing us into the area of themata.*

Certainly, interpretation in general is not a specifically philosophical task (the above interpretations need chess players, not philosophers, to make and assess them), though the rivals among the more holistic interpretative systems (such as Marxism and psychoanalysis) certainly pose philosophical problems.

Yet there remains the task of discerning general features of interpretation, both formally (as in work done in formal semantics), and through discussion of the leading notion of a thema (a discussion which the present annex is intended to display rather than conclude).

10 Styles of Life

We have now the abstract apparatus to account for that feature of sets of values which we called their style. For sets of values may be unified by their thematic structure, the simplest case being that in which all the appetita convey the same thema.

But this formal anwer is exceedingly bare. What kinds of thematic structure are there? What determines them? What limits are set upon them? How can we set about that work of interpretation which would elicit the thematic structure of a particular set of values?

(xi) Human Nature

There is one strategy here which has been widespread in moral philosophy: we set out to discover an anchor for human values independent of what men happen to desire. This anchor is often found in 'human nature'.

It may be argued, for instance, that men's needs or interests are objectively determinable, independently of what they may desire. Such needs or interests will then be held to have a determining role at least for some parts of human value systems, and to set limits upon them. This position is all the more in need of consideration since we have not yet made any mention of needs or interests.

From the point of view of our argument, the leading question is whether needs or interests could indeed be established independently of desires. We should distinguish four theses at this point:

(1) that it is possible to establish what a particular man's interests are independently of what his desires are;

(2) that it is possible to establish what human interests are independently of human desires;

(3) that it is possible to establish what human interests are on the basis of some general facts about human nature;

(4) that it is possible to establish what ought and ought not to be done mediately or immediately on the basis of human interests.

We shall consider these theses in turn. It will be convenient to allow the term 'desire' to cover the whole class of what I have called appetitives, and to consider only interests, on the supposition that closely analogous considerations will apply to appetitives other than wanting, and to needs as well as interests.

There are several versions of the first thesis:

(a) that it is possible to establish what a particular man's interests are independently of any particular desire of his (i.e. a desire for **x** is never sufficient ground for saying **x** is in his interest);

76

*(b) that it is possible to establish what a particular man's interests are independently of the totality of his desires at any particular time (i.e. his total aversion to **x** now is never sufficient ground for saying that **x** is not in his interest);*

(c) that it is possible to establish what a particular man's interests are independently of all his desires.

The first two versions of the first thesis (together with corresponding versions of the second) are entirely plausible. It is the third version which we shall question. Could we reasonably say that something was in a person's interest even though it neither matched nor helped the attainment of any of his desires, then or later? It may be said that saving the life of a would-be suicide is doing something in his interest, whatever his desires may be, now or in the future. But what if for the rest of his life he regrets and resents his survival?

'You say that I am at least alive: yet life holds nothing for me. You say that securing my survival is securing an interest of mine: but in that case my interest has become a technical and biological condition to which I am indifferent. My life is not my survival. . . .'

Yet this is only one example, and we may find in Mill's satisfied pig and in his dissatisfied Socrates a plausible example suggesting the independence of a particular man's interests from the totality of his desires. For a vegetable life which answered grosso modo to the totality of a man's actual desires would yet not be in his interest if he had latent and unexplored talents, even if the exploitation of those talents might produce suffering and discontent. It seems to me that this sort of case—and indeed that of the suicide—is precisely a matter of dispute: of moral dispute. In other words, if we are inclined to accept Mill's view, it is in the light of our own values. It is not, therefore, an example that can settle the issue: for a person holding, as I would, that interests are not independent of desires may simply observe that the term 'interest' in this example may have one of two functions: either it is camouflage (in saying what is in this man's interest, I really mean that I want men in general and this man in particular to develop their talents), or it involves tacit reference to hypothetical desires of that man (I say that it is in his interest to develop his talents not only because so will he better serve his desires, but because if now per impossibile he could make an informed choice, he would desire the development of his talents and not their atrophy, and correspondingly would, if they were not developed—and if per impossibile he were able to appreciate what he had not experienced—regret it).

The corresponding third version of the second thesis, that it is possible to *establish what human interests are independently of the totality of human desires, is even harder to accept. If then we must reject the first and second theses, at least in this strong form, we shall be in a position to reject the view that interests are primary, and to argue that they are on the contrary secondary to desires. The topic of interests would then be a subordinate theme within the appetitive framework already proposed (and our strategy would in outline be this—to analyse consulting the interests of* **a** *as desiring the state of affairs in which* **p**, *and in which—because* **p**—*certain desires of* **a** *are more readily fulfilled).*

However, the attempt to subordinate an account of interests to the general account of value and desire offered here may be countered by the third thesis, that interests are established not on the basis of human desires, but on the basis of human nature. But now we are confronted by a range of Thomistic problems. Will it not be the nature of all things to seek the good? How, then, could we distinguish basing interests on desires from basing them on human nature? Some have envisaged facts about the nature of the human organism such that certain things are necessary to its survival, so that anything which procures or safeguards those things could be said to be to that extent in man's interest. But why should the survival of individual men have a determining role for human interests, especially since men are in any case mortal? With what justice can one say (appealing to such considerations) that it would be in the interest of the peoples of the Indian sub-continent if the sacred cow were desacrified? One would mean, of course, that a more 'rational' livestock policy would contribute to the elimination of famine, which brings suffering and death to many people. But those people themselves may hold that survival at that cost cannot be in their interest. . . . There is a genuine conflict of values here: it cannot be resolved by a straightforward appeal to supposedly objective interests.

Thus theses (1) to (3) seem to me to be misleading or false, though thesis (4), which would give a role to interests (or needs) in the grounding of moral notions, seems to me to be unexceptionable. It is, however, a thesis which can be accommodated within the general structure of our present argument, so long as it is not held that interests be ascertained independently of desires.

In any case, it should by now be rather clear that even if accounts relying on the independence of needs or interests could be established, they would not provide a means of accounting for what we have called 'style' in value systems. Rather they would tend to show a basic core within different styles of value. They would separate two kinds of value: the first an indispensable minimum, a critical or social morality thought of as providing a necessary framework for human life, within which the second kind of value—total value systems with their differing ideals and styles—would appear as it were as 'options': a matter for man's free choice. And here we confront a certain philosophical obsession; or a certain obsession of philosophy: the obsession with man.

Lévi-Strauss detects this obsession in existentialism, which he describes as 'an exercise in self-admiration in which contemporary man is duped, shut up in colloquy with himself, prostrate in extasy before himself. It is cut off from scientific knowledge which is despised, and genuine humanity whose historical depth and ethnographical dimensions are not recognised, in order to set up a closed and private world: an ideological Café du Commerce where the habitués, safely inside the four walls of a human condition made to the measure of a specific society, all day long go over problems of local interest, beyond which the smoky atmosphere of their dialectical fug prevents them from seeing' (1971, p. 572). Again, more generally, Michel Foucault has outlined the historical appearance of that configuration of knowledge which constitutes man as a central but problematic object: that which is studied by several sciences, but never fully—a being in the end impermeable to science. Foucault forecasts the erasure from our universe of this enigmatic outline which is man, like the face in the sand which is obliterated by an incoming tide.

The point of these observations seems to be as follows. Western philosophy, since the moment of Socrates's rejection of the sciences of nature, has never ceased to construct defences against science, by attempting to appropriate or exploit its findings, by attempting to discredit it on philosophical grounds, or—as a last resort—by attempting to secure an area as the proper preserve of philosophy, the enclosure taking a different form according to each advance of knowledge which philosophy, in her reactionary guise, takes to be a new encroachment. Thus we find philosophers—nomads whose title to land for grazing always yields to advancing sedentary communities which cultivate the land—occupying temporary camps in various corners of the intellectual universe. The boundary of one such camp is staked out by the 'problem of the freedom of the will': in this camp, a central part of the study of man is reserved for philosophy. Another camp is delimited by the currently widespread view of philosophy as concerned with 'conceptual problems'. On this view, the distinction between conceptual and empirical truths is held to be axiomatic, and conceptual problems are supposed to be susceptible only to a specific kind of non-empirical investigation, that of the philosopher.

So do we set man outside nature, detecting that peculiar position in his consciousness, his freedom, his concepts or his language: in his ability to apprehend, through philosophy, a realm of necessity distinct from the natural order. And so our first question to the present schematic account of value and *desire is: how does man come out of it? Is he absolutely unconditioned, free to will what he will? What determines values, and what limits them? These are questions with the wrong spin, when they are thought of as philosophical questions. In fact, they are scientific questions, and what is said in this book is a schematic part of an ethnology, a sociology, a psychology, an ethology, a biology, a cybernetics, as much as part of a 'philosophy'; it should be read as advocating the destruction of the boundary fences between these fields, or rather as urging a recognition that the boundaries which they are intended to mark are in a number of important respects illusory.*

10 Styles of Life

Returning to the style of value systems—to forms of life—we are chastened: the substantial claims about what constitutes them are to be found in the various sciences, and such claims are beyond our present scope. That section of our main argument which would show its point turns out to be empty. However, the formal account offered of styles in value systems in terms of a common thematic structure enables us to see how particular claims of this kind would take their place in our general account of values.

One thing is very clear, that we are placed at some distance from conventional moral philosophy. For certainly what is comprised in a style of life or of values goes much beyond what has come to be thought of as a matter of morality. For the Greeks, by contrast, it was quite natural that the aristocratic style of life marked by magnificence should be a topic in moral treatises. On our terms too, the inclusion of such a topic would be entirely appropriate.

But we are faced again with the strong tradition of the autonomy of moral concepts: is it wholly erroneous? What are the special features of 'moral values'? Indeed, more generally, what species of value are there?

11 Species of Value

It may seem that since the present account purports to deal with all values by referring them to corresponding desires, no justice can be done to the insights of those who have insisted on the autonomy of moral values, or the special character, for instance, of aesthetic values. To take a more specific objection of the same kind, it may seem that no justice can be done to cases described and experienced as cases of conflict between a moral principle and a desire.

The specific objection is rather easily countered. For if having a moral principle is itself having a desire of a particular kind, there will be no more difficulty in accounting for conflicts of the kind in question than for any other cases of conflicting desires. But even if this be granted, we may still ask what kind of desire constitutes having a moral principle.

It is in the end a historical and sociological question why and how some distinctions between kinds of value receive greater emphasis and attention in a particular society or period than in another. The existence of a wide range of discriminations between kinds of value has been discussed at some length in section 7. It remains to show how a sufficient characterisation of what may broadly be called a contemporary Western notion of moral as opposed to other values may be given in terms of these distinctions, though it must be remembered that this characterisation is not only subject to correction by the historian or social scientist, but is also a characterisation of something which is itself subject to change, so that views according to which moral values are autonomous are displayed as in that respect mere rationalisations of local prejudice.

Moral values, then, may be characterised as follows, using the distinctions of section 7: they are *primary* (involving a commitment to action); they are *real* (for the hypocrite, for instance, is precisely one who does not believe in the moral value in question); they are *open* (for closed values lack the universality taken to be an important feature of moral values); they may be either *positive* or *negative* (we are perhaps witnessing a historical change of emphasis from negative to positive values); they are *architectonic* or *higher order* values (for lower order values, especially first-order ones, do not have the intrinsic feature of regulating other values, a regulation which introduces all kinds of disciplines from rule-following to spiritual exercises, and which is important in morality); they are *absolute* (for morality is thought of as independent of the at least partly selfish concerns represented by relative desires).

This characterisation of 'moral values' should not be thought of as a theory of morality. Nor would there be any purpose served by testing and challenging each of the offered criteria in turn. For if, for instance, one said, 'But it is not *necessary* to morality that every value be "primary" in your sense', the reply is that there is no necessity here. There is a cultural and historical evolution in values, a particular configuration of which in modern Western society is in fact relatively distinct from other values, is thought of as such, and is moreover called by this special name: 'morality'.

But the description of that configuration given above, is a description of one of many possible different kinds of configuration, which is to say possible species of value; of these possible species many have also existed, which is to say, acquired currency as lived distinctions. We have known law-style moralities, and corresponding theories of morality, which give a special place to negative values; utilitarian moralities and theories of morality, which give a special place to tertiary values (those maximised satisfactions taken to be the final measure); moral theories and moralities giving a special place to universality (such as Christian or Islamic as opposed to say, Judaic moralities), and which in our terms emphasise absolute and open values; deontological theories of morality and moralities in which duties take first place, which lay emphasis on architectonic values; teleological and technical value systems (not only moralities) which draw attention to the internal 'instrumental' structure of appetitives discussed in annex (vii) above; aesthetic values, which are tertiary values primarily concerned with human artefacts, or what can paronymously be treated as such.

All these and many other configurations of human values call us insistently away from the abstractions governing the present argument. To suspend them completely is to let our theory rejoin our practice. Indeed, the abstraction which permits theory to emerge can be vindicated nowhere else.

(xii) Neutrality in Moral Philosophy

A. J. Ayer writes that any theory of morality

'*is entirely on the level of analysis; it is an attempt to show what people are doing when they make moral judgements; it is not a set of suggestions as to what moral judgements they are to make. And this is true of all moral philosophy as I understand it. All moral theories . . . in so far as they are philosophical theories, are neutral as regards actual conduct.*' *(1959, pp. 245–6)*

The remarks just offered should make it clear that this is a misleading view. For it supposes that in morality we are dealing with a given phenomenon in human behaviour which we could thus attempt to observe, describe and analyse impartially. But rival views about what is essential to morality do not offer, whatever the appearances, different accounts of the same configuration of phenomena: they draw attention to, or even create different configurations. Groups differ, not only in their moral beliefs, but also in their conceptions of what constitutes morality, if indeed they have any distinction between moral and other values.

Moral philosophy can only hope for a degree of neutrality by taking its place as a difficult branch of general value theory: such is the argument of this book. But if it is correct, and if this degree of neutrality is possible, the important reproach levelled at neutralist moral philosophies comes into play, that they admit, or even licence and encourage, any abhorrent and aberrant position, on the sole condition that some formal requirements be met.

12 The Evaluation of Values

How then will our theory rejoin our practice? Will it not be assimilable into *any* practice? Will it not sanction *any* wilful action? Does it not at least imply that there could be no rational basis for condemning any action? If by *rational basis* is meant some set of principles from which it could be deduced or cogently argued that such and such an action is wrong, independently of any desires of the person making the judgement or of some other person involved, then indeed there can be no rational basis for such condemnation. Condemnation can only be based upon a value.

Of course, there is the possibility of the evaluation or assessment of values not with a view to praise or blame, acceptance or rejection, but *technically*: we may discuss their practicability, their scope, their compatibility and compracticability with other values, their internal structure, and so on. It is in this way that much moral discourse, practical and theoretical, turns out to be technical. But we can and do also assess values morally—we evaluate them. In so doing we are adopting or expressing another value. But when a conflict arises, how can it be settled? Since what we are dealing with is in the end a conflict of desires, that conflict can only be settled by one or both of the parties abandoning or modifying his desire, or having it overriden. Indeed, moral debate is essentially the attempt of one or both parties to it to bring the other to recognise that he does not really want what he thought he wanted, or if he does, to change this desire. And it proceeds by such techniques as drawing out the consequences of a desire, appealing to some commonly held value, and showing that it applies to the case in spite of appearances. The latter technique is merely a special case of showing that something does fall under a certain concept. There is nothing to be said for giving it a special name (such as 'universalisability') and claiming it to be a distinguishing feature of moral discourse; nor is there anything to be said for a revision of this position by which universalisability is held to mark all descriptive terms, but to have a particular importance in the case of moral terms, since they also have 'prescriptive meaning' enabling us to infer imperatives.

Indeed, concentration upon the meaning of moral judgements is a poor starting point in moral philosophy. For too many important questions have to be begged in assuming in advance a clear and agreed distinction between moral judgements and others. On our account, value judgements in general will be any judgements to the effect that some value is or is not satisfied (that is, that the propositions in the corresponding appetitum are or are not true). Around this central case will be a variety of peripheral cases in which a more indirect appeal to a value must be made in understanding a judgement, where something, for instance, is judged conducive to or symptomatic of the satisfaction of some value. If the value entering into a judgement is that of the person making the judgement, he does have some commitment to action, because of the nature of values, but not because of the meaning of the judgement. For instance, a value may come into play not only in transforming the world, but also in measuring it. When the world is measured and comes up to scratch, no action is called for; but the meaning of some judgement which was once a guide to action, and is now the sign of its successful completion, does not change. Values may find expression in prescriptions, but value judgements do not have a special kind of meaning called prescriptive meaning.

The ways in which values enter into the meaning of terms is a complex topic which has been well opened up by Julius Kovesi (1967). But considerations of meaning do not enter into the evaluation of values. If I say that I think that the exploitation of the weak, the defenceless and the poor is wrong, this can only mean that I do not want them to be exploited, can only mean a fight against the desires which contribute to that exploitation, even if they are found in myself.

This view may be a threat to the morality which is aloofly consciousness of the truth of its pronouncements, but it leaves in clear view the morality which is a practical commitment to a different world, which is the work of men of good will.

13 The End

Throughout this book, we have argued good to be the end of all human striving—we have composed an extended footnote to the ancient definition of the good as 'that for which all things strive'. But in so doing, we have consistently taken the existence of desires to be the fundamental datum. That certain desires exist has been the brute fact; we have neither asked for nor allowed explanations of their existence. Such questions lay beyond the metaphysical limits of our position. Putting it more brutally, 'I just want it' has been made the final word in all questions of value. Is this not an infantile and anarchic position? Why should desires exist at all, and why should those desires exist which do? Why should we ever expect ourselves to be able to persuade others of the desirability of certain states of affairs?

Let us return to our model universe with one will. Why should that will produce some one change rather than another? In a revised version of the model (pp. 47–8), we were led to say that the 'intention' or 'appetitum' which appears in that zone of the universe which is the will's is not attributable, or that it can be attributed to no agency other than that of the will. It is this arbitrariness present in the original model which has persisted throughout our account and which is now being challenged.

Let us note that further consideration of our model universe may itself impose that challenge. For if we allow it to be arbitrary what the will in that universe directs itself towards, what distinction will remain between a change produced by the will, and a change occurring spontaneously? Indeed, etymologically, 'spontaneous' means 'willed'. On the other hand, if we try to escape arbitrariness by allowing determinations of the will from outside, then the will ceases to be a source of change, and the distinction between a change produced by it and a change produced by previous changes will also collapse.

This is a dilemma apparent in the confrontation between executive/mechanistic and voluntarist views of choice, between an Aristotelian view of choice as the putting into effect of pre-existing policies, and an existentialist view of choice as the sovereign creation of policy. Ricœur's attempt at a compromise between these positions (1950) seems to me to be unsuccessful. The dilemma, which seems to require us to take one of two positions, each of which is unacceptable, arises from certain underlying assumptions about the will. These assumptions are made plain in our model universe, and it is there that we shall most fruitfully consider how the will could remain distinguishable from what we called spontaneous events on the one hand, and from deterministic series of events on the other.

There seem to be two lines of solution to this problem. The first is to abjure completely the transcendental residue in our revised model universe. We have already noticed in annex (viii) above that on the interpretation of the 'zone of the will' in our model, the will must be other than and outside all the items in that zone: it will transcend the universe: it will be that 'centre of the world' of which Wittgenstein speaks in the passage which forms an epigraph to this book. We shall now simply identify the will with its zone. The description of that zone will tend towards and should merge into the theory of self-regulating organisms, and the way forward will be with the sciences dealing with such organisms.

But is this solution merely an adoption of the mechanistic horn of the dilemma? To suggest that this may not be so, we must look rather far afield.

For long the understanding of the universe, and the solution of particular problems about it, depended upon the drawing of boundaries in experience which would clearly delimit and abstract the entities concerned and the area of study, within a universe conceived as a single, globally determined whole. These boundaries were of such a kind as to delimit closed systems: that is, they were not permeable boundaries. Thus Newtonian mechanics deals essentially with closed dynamic systems. In a particular problem concerning such and such bodies, the influence of other bodies on the system cannot be taken into account at all, except indirectly, by being transmuted into so many special forces considered as acting within the system in question. The success of Newtonian mechanics is all the more remarkable when we consider that it is unable to deal with systems of more than two bodies, except by *ad hoc* methods of approximation, and that it was obliged to multiply special forces again in a very *ad hoc* fashion.

Thus the other face of the tremendous and fruitful simplification of problems achieved by this approach is a tremendous complexity of solutions of actual problems, or indeed the unavailability of solutions except by *ad hoc* procedures in all but the simplest cases.

One method of dealing with complexities of this kind is to treat the phenomena within the closed system under consideration statistically. In a sense, then, it becomes unimportant that there are questions that cannot, in principle or in practice, be answered about the behaviour of particular particles in the system or about their interaction. We now confront that triumph of closed system thinking: classical thermodynamics. But it is a triumph gained in the teeth of life. For the phenomena of life, at the level of the particular organism, or at the level of the evolutionary process, present remarkable and consistent examples of the maintenance of highly improbable states, and of their regular evolution in the direction of even greater complexity and improbability.

Now the Newtonian model exemplifies a pattern of enquiry and thought which is in no way restricted to physics, and it may be useful to summarise its leading features:

(1) items are considered only as belonging to *closed systems*, though the closure need not restrict us to a finite number of items, nor need it necessarily be considered to represent a closure in the nature of things, rather than being one convenient application of a methodological necessity—to restrict our field of enquiry (this pattern can be widely detected, from literary criticism and chemistry to formal semantics);

(2) the items of a systems are *atoms* of it—within that system they cannot be decomposed or explained, and if they behave differently from each other, this has to be treated as a brute fact (in classical chemistry, the elements have to be atomistically conceived in this way, but again we are dealing with a widespread pattern of thought, from economics to folk-lore);

(3) the interactions of items within a system are governed by laws, forces or constants which can be ascertained but not explained from within (such as gravity in classical dynamics, or Grimm's Law in philology);

(4) the overlapping of systems may occur and occur systematically, but this is only where a new system can be envisaged comprising both earlier systems (such would be the case for an envisaged collapse of chemistry into physics); otherwise overlaps have to be treated as arbitrary or merely coincidental.

Indisputably, all these features of classical science, indeed of classical thought, have been very fruitful. But they are all open to question. We may begin with the fourth feature—with overlap problems. Jacques Monod has written:

> In roulette, uncertainty is operational and not essential. . . . But in other situations the notion of chance takes on an essential and not purely operational significance. This is so, for instance, of what may be called 'absolute coincidences', that is, those which result from the intersection of two *totally independent* causal chains. Suppose that Dr. Smith has an emergency call to visit a patient, while Jones the plumber is carrying out an emergency repair to the roof of a nearby building. When Dr. Smith passes at the foot of the building, the ↗plumber inadvertently drops his hammer the (deterministic) trajectory of which intersects that of the doctor who dies of a fractured skull. We say that it was bad luck. What other word could we use for such an event, unforeseeable *by its very nature*? It is clear that chance here must be considered as playing an essential role, inherent in the *total independence* of the two series of events whose interaction produces the accident (1970, p. 128: my italics).

Now the notion of absolute coincidence is an inevitable corollary of the closed system approach; for if two systems of events intersect but are quite distinct, then *ex hypothesi* there is no system within which that intersection could be explained.

We may remember Evans-Pritchard's well-known description of Zande beliefs:

> In Zandeland sometimes an old granary collapses. There is nothing remarkable in this. Every Zande knows that termites eat the supports in course of time, and that even the hardest woods decay after years of service. Now a granary is the summerhouse of a Zande homestead, and people sit beneath it in the heat of the day and chat or play the African hole-game or work at some craft. Consequently it may happen that there are people sitting beneath the granary when it collapses and they are injured, for it is a heavy structure made of beams and clay and may be stored with eleusine as well. Now why should these particular people have been sitting under this particular granary at the particular moment when it collapsed? That it should collapse is easily intelligible, but why should it have collapsed at the particular moment when these particular people were sitting beneath it? Through years it might

have collapsed, so why should it fall just when certain people sought its kindly shelter? We say that the granary collapsed because its supports were eaten away by termites. That is the cause that explains the collapse of the granary. We also say that people were sitting under it at the time because it was in the heat of the day and they thought that it would be a comfortable place to talk and work. This is the cause of people being under the granary at the time it collapsed. To our minds the only relationship between these two *independently caused* facts is their coincidence in time and space. We have no explanation of why the *two chains of causation* intersected at a certain time and in a certain place, for there is no interdependence between them. Zande philosophy can supply the missing link. The Zande knows that the supports were undermined by termites and that people were sitting beneath the granary in order to escape the heat and glare of the sun. But he knows besides why these two events occurred at a precisely similar moment in time and space. It was due to the action of witchcraft. If there had been no witchcraft people would have been sitting under the granary and it would not have fallen on them, or it would have collapsed but the people would not have been sheltering under it at the time. Witchcraft explains the coincidence of these two happenings. (1937, pp. 69–70, my italics)

It is not my purpose here to construct any argument intended to suggest that the Azande may be right in their beliefs about witchcraft. The point rather is that Monod finds it natural in presenting and justifying an important methodological assumption—which results in a belief in absolute coincidence—to appeal to what seems plain common sense. But the Zande example shows what Descartes was neither the first nor the last to point out, that though common sense may be regarded as a common possession human opinions may nevertheless differ, and differ on the most fundamental assumptions.

The appeal to common sense here, as everywhere, is therefore unsatisfactory. It is open to us—indeed, incumbent upon us—to challenge any belief in 'totally independent causal chains', and therefore in 'absolute coincidence'. That the creator of relativity theory—a decisive break from classical science—should have been reluctant to accept the uncertainty principle (to believe that 'God plays at dice') is itself not a coincidence: for the belief in *absolute coincidence* is as ineluctable a feature of classical thought as the belief in absolute space and time. What positive form such a challenge might take we shall consider shortly. Meanwhile, it is enough to observe that the appeal to coincidence which is a corollary of the closed system approach when different systems overlap is a reason for discomfort.

If we now turn to the forces, constants and laws which are appealed to to explain events occurring within the system, there too we find cause for unease: for such principles, lying at the metaphysical limits of such a system, are incapable of explanation from within it. Valency for example is an essential concept of classical chemistry. The attribution of valencies to the elements is a necessary condition for the description and explanation of chemical reaction. Yet there can be no chemical explanation of differences of valency. Again, in biology, the old dispute between mechanistic and vitalist views of life was metaphysical shadow boxing, since the disputants commonly shared a closed system approach: consequently, the principles appealed to in accounting for biological systems were not open to biological explanation.

What has happened in such cases has commonly been the establishment or envisaging of a wider system; or at least the appeal to another system. Valency receives an explanation in physics; and phenomena of life may be held to receive their explanation in chemistry. We begin to glimpse a hierarchical and possibly reductionist view of the structure of science. But the urge to reductionism is itself a kind of challenge to the classical approach; here also, then, we should be ready to question that approach.

We may now turn to the next feature of the approach, its atomism. It is not only the dark areas of Wittgenstein's *Tractatus* that should give us pause here: in many sciences the view of systems as composed of independently identifiable items which interact is proving unsatisfactory. Phonetics is powerless if it attempts to give an independent acoustic definition of each sound in a language, and then tries to ascertain how such items may be combined. Studies of folk-lore are sterile if they stay with Stith Thompson's or even Propp's lists of folk-tale components. Physics has long ceased to be a straightforward study of corpuscular interactions.

Finally, if we turn to the leading notion of the approach from which its other features stem—that we should always regard ourselves as treating closed systems—there is every reason to hesitate once more. For the most obvious examples around us—biological systems—are obviously and essentially *not* closed: they depend upon and are characterised by the exchange of matter and of energy with their environment.

If we detect a challenge to classical thought on all these fronts, what positive form may this challenge take? We shall approach this question by adverting briefly to contemporary movements in mathematics, biology, social anthropology and linguistics.

There is a recent movement in mathematics arising from the work of the Bourbaki and calling itself category theory. According to this view, the segmentation of mathematics into a number of sub-disciplines each dealing with its own kind of system is harmful and intellectually malfounded. We start with the existence of structural homologies between different (including widely different) mathematical sub-disciplines, and treat them by a kind of general theory of homology reminiscent of the technical homology theory of topology, but perfectly general in scope. Mathematics is one: and not in the traditional sense whereby we attempt to show that all the (admittedly different) branches can be variously traced to the one set-theoretic root, but by appealing to structure rather than foundations, and showing that these 'branches' are varyingly homologous systems of transformation themselves transformed in accordance with a general theory of such transformations.

This movement offers the perspective of a radical challenge to the disciplinarity which is a feature of the traditional approach in the sciences (and elsewhere): and not a challenge which would proceed by praising attempts at 'interdisciplinary' cooperation. If we accept the traditional notion of disciplines *at all*, crossing of the boundaries in any systematic way is impossible: there is no intellectual space for such commuting. Each kind of closed system is a separate object of study: at the overlaps we find brute coincidence, and any apparent analogies between different systems are themselves haphazard; to give them serious attention would be intellectually disreputable: at best they may provide flashes of insight like electrical discharges occurring at random, and flashes of insight whose only justification can lie in their proper incorporation in the receiving discipline.

Thus category theory enables us to conceive the possibility that where traditionally two 'disciplines' were separated by an imperme-able boundary, they now emerge as linked by one or more specific articulations or hinges on the one hand, and perhaps display some perfect continuities or abrupt discontinuities on the other. If this is so in a particular case, the emergence of analogous structures in what we used to think of as the two domains will no longer be a coincidence, a 'mere metaphor'. In particular 'absolute coincidence' will disappear, since there will no longer be 'absolutely independent causal chains';

rather the independence of causal patterns will be strictly relative to the structural relations between the domains in which they are displayed.

In addition to such challenges to disciplinarity, there are more direct challenges to the appeal to closed systems, in particular those associated with the name of von Bertalanffy in biology. Bertalanffy has argued that we cannot deal with biological phenomena adequately unless we recognise that we are dealing with open systems, namely, those in which there may be exchange of matter and energy with the environment. Such systems are capable of rigorous treatment, and there are flourishing programmes of research in the area for instance of non-equilibrium thermodynamics (such as the work of the Brussels school under Prigogine). They show a number of special characteristics. In the first place, they may maintain themselves in a state of high statistical improbability, a steady state different from the classical thermodynamic equilibrium. Secondly, they may display what Bertalanffy calls 'equifinality', a property by which the steady state, if reached, is effectively independent of the initial conditions of the system, being determined by its parameters. The notion of open systems (of which cybernetic systems, or 'Ashby machines' displaying negative feedback, and open only to information and not energy exchange, are special cases) is fruitful not only in biology, in studies of growth and metabolism, genetics and evolution (where it allows us to envisage a new turn to the acrid disputes over nature/nurture distinctions), but also in the suggestive power of a 'general systems theory' in a variety of other areas.

Finally, we may consider direct challenges to classical atomism. These are perhaps most clearly displayed in social anthropology and linguistics, where 'structuralist' movements are precisely characterised by their refusal to take the elements in the field under study as given items of which it may independently be ascertained that they occur in such and such combinations and not others. On the contrary, it is held that the identity of an element is determined only by its place in the system. In phonetics, for instance, a vowel is the vowel it is not because of the physically measurable nature of the sound emitted, but because of the constitutive systems of relations between sounds which are the phonetics of a given language. In the case of studies of folklore, we find Vladimir Propp writing (although he is supposed to be a forerunner of structuralism): 'The total number of elements, the constituent parts of fairy tales, is about one hundred and fifty. . . . While in biology, a change in one part or characteristic entails the changing of another characteristic, in the tale, any part can change independently of the others. . . . We may conclude, then, the constituent parts can be studied out of context of the story which they compose.' Propp's resolute atomism in this area seems inherently unconvincing: at all events, its inadequacy is sufficiently demonstrated by Lévi-Strauss's *Mythologiques*.

We glimpse here emerging severally in different branches of knowledge what may in due course be recognised as a new organon. The formal theory of this organon may be emerging most dramatically in the work of René Thom, whose qualitative dynamics would have two important consequences from the point of view of the arguments of this book: first, the reinstatement of certain analogues of teleological explanation for local processes, and secondly, the rejection of a Laplacian belief in global determinism in favour of a characterisation of science—including the human sciences—as concerned to discover and analyse local determinisms within a generally rather labile and chaotic universe. Among such local determinisms there would indeed be found those which we have called 'wills': but a rigorous description of them through an appropriate science need no longer commit us to a traditional mechanistic view. Moreover we may well have no special reason to adopt that conventional philosophical position known as reductionism, by which the apparent autonomy of the human will would be reduced to some other globally deterministic level of explanation.

In short, there may be emerging new configurations of knowledge in which, on the one hand, classically severe disciplinary distinctions will disappear, and, on the other, the study of 'wills'—that is, of active self-regulating organisms, of autonomous but not closed systems—will have strategic importance. It is beyond my present purpose and competence to give a serious review of these developments; yet they are connected with that model universe which was constructed in section 1, and has guided the whole argument of this book. They are developments, moreover, which have other specific bearings upon our arguments.

Paronymy, for instance, was a notion indispensable in our treatment of wishing and of pleasure. And it emerged as an intractable notion. But the possibility of general theories of homology at a formal level (such as in category theory), and of specific treatments of specific homologies made possible by the replacement of disciplinary boundaries by disciplinary articulations, opens up the prospect of challenging the basis of that definition of paronymy which gave it a questionable and mysterious status: namely, the assumption (particularly dubious in the psychological case which was our first concern) that there really are *different* domains, where *difference* would connote incommensurability, and paronymy would be the transfer of a term from one to the other, a paradoxical transfer supposed to take place in the absence of any space in which it could be effected.

Pleasure, for instance, was argued to be homologous to wanting for a domain in which (unlike that of wanting) the desired state of affairs is taken to be already present. Now the existence of this homology (already recognised in a formal notion such as that of the 'pro-attitude', since the presence of a pro-attitude could be manifested indifferently in any of our three modes) is able to be set in the context of a general possibility of detecting such homologies, where different domains are accessible to each other through regular transformations of their defining conditions.

Moreover, our divagations in this section give us a glimpse of a biological homology of the psychological want/pleasure relation already alluded to in annex (iv). An open system of Bertalanffy may have parameters tending to keep it in a steady state distinct from classical thermodynamic equilibrium. This has two consequences; one, that the system is 'naturally' active (it displays autonomous activity), and secondly, that if a case occurs in which that activity is anticipated in its goal by other forces, then that activity, directed at producing a state which already exists, is superfluous and forms an 'overshoot' (see Bertalanffy, 1968, p. 143). The existence of such a biological analogue of what pleasure would be on the account offered in section 4 above is an important consideration, and should not be dismissed as a *mere* analogy: for man *is* a biological organism: we have envisaged an organon in which psychology and biology would emerge as structurally linked domains.

Thus, to return from this rather dizzying detour, the rejection of the transcendental interpretation of the 'zone of the will' in our model universe, and the corresponding identification of the will with that zone, will not necessarily commit us to a classical mechanistic view of what we should in that case scarcely be entitled any longer to call 'will': the mechanistic/voluntaristic dilemma which we outlined has now taken a different form. Our problem was whether the three classifications of changes in our model universe of section 1 could be kept distinct. In particular, could the 'will' be distinguished from changes attributable to causal chains, and changes attributable to nothing (or to chance)? The tendency of our observations has been that the classical distinction between chance and necessity (from Democritus to Jacques Monod) is simply a feature of an obsolescent ideology of science. Under a rival approach, the admission of mechanism and chance to our model universe will be seen as misleading: the autonomous action of a system (call it 'the will') is a starting point: it is the extrapolations (if they are such) to pure mechanistic causal chains, or to pure chance, which now become problematic. On this rival approach, man remains a natural phenomenon, but his ends belong to a teleology susceptible of treatment in a configuration of the sciences made possible by their escape from the old dilemma—chance or necessity, a dilemma which received schematic form in our model.

But there is another view, in which man appears also in a supernatural world. Teilhard de Chardin wrote:

> I have observed that for the best of unbelievers morality comes down to the precept 'do not do to others what you would not wish them to do to you'. This morality, in my opinion, is anodyne and static. It oils the wheels, but it is not enough. The human machine must do more than not squeak. It needs energy or fuel. This energy, this essence (that is, being obliged to act, or having the taste for action)—it is the whole problem of morality to provide. Now I see no other possible source than submission to a universal ideal object (*believed in* and *hoped for*, but not tangible; for it is universal and in the future, while we are individuals and in the present). (1965, pp. 53–4).

On this view, recognition of teleology places human striving in necessary relation to a transcendental goal—the forms of Plato, the non-natural goodness of G. E. Moore, the Divinity as the end of all ends, though like the case of immanent causality discussed above, transcendent causality too will take on a quite different form in a structuralist/open system perspective. Indeed, will the two coincide?

We may start once more from the necessary presence to the will in our model universe of a projection of a possible change. It is this *being directed towards* a possible future state of affairs that is characteristic of the will. Can we account for such directedness merely by reference to a tendency to produce the end? Why *should* the will tend to produce it? One reply might be that ends are not made so by being aimed at: they are aimed at because they already present themselves as ends—as an imperfect reflection of the one End.

But is there any longer a distinction between that End as a perfection beyond our striving and as contained within it? Such speculation is the beginning of many books (most of which have not been written): of this one, it is—the end.

Summary of the
Main Argument

Defining the will as a source of change does not entitle us to exclude the possibility of the frustration of the will. The source of values schematically lies in the possible failure of the world to match the project of a will.

There are three chief modes of the will in man: first, wanting (determined by three criteria—the conative, there being a tendency to action; the prospective, this action being aimed at bringing about some state of affairs in the future; and the propositional, there being some set of propositions which the wanter is trying to make true); secondly, wishing (in which the same criteria are satisfied, save that the conative criterion is only paronymously satisfied); and thirdly, taking pleasure in something (in which the same criteria are satisfied, save that the conative and prospective criteria are only paronymously satisfied).

Any psychological state falling under this general account may be called an appetitive, and the object upon which an appetitive is directed may be called an appetitum. Any appetitum is a value, in accordance with which the world is to be changed, or by which it may be measured.

Values may be classified according to the corresponding appetitive structure. They may be primary, secondary or tertiary (according to the three broad classes of appetitives); they may be real or quasi-values (according to whether the value in question is a value of the person in question, or the person merely acts as though it were a value of his); they may be open or closed (according to whether or not they could be finally satisfied); they may be positive or negative; they may be first order, higher order or architectonic (according to whether other values figure essentially in the appetitum); they may be relative or absolute (according to whether or not reference to the person whose value it is occurs essentially in the appetitum).

In addition, values may be classified according to the reference group, that is the group of people whose values they are. Here there are three cases: values which are possessed by only one individual, values which are shared, and values which belong primarily to a collectivity.

Further, values may form systems, by compresence (being held together by the same person or group of persons), by compatibility or compracticability (being logically or practically able to be achieved together), and by style (forming together what is, by some criterion, a coherent picture of a possible future world).

Within this general framework, different species of value can be discerned. The number of possible combinations of the distinctions given is very large, but only certain configurations acquire or are given importance (such as the configuration called 'morality' or 'aesthetics'). Which they are and why they are is finally a historical and sociological question.

Values can be assessed technically (having in view their practicability, their scope, their compatibility and compracticability with other values, their internal structure, and so on). We may also assess a value evaluatively, but only by accepting some value which will act as a basis of that evaluation.

If we ask why do those values exist which do, there are two possible answers, one that it is the life sciences (and only they) which can give and are in fact giving the answer; and secondly, a transcendental view according to which certain ends of themselves attract our desire.

Bibliography

There follows a selective list of books which I have referred to or made use of.

Aristotle, *De Interpretatione*
—— *Nicomachean Ethics*
Ayer, A. J., *Philosophical Essays* (London, 1959)
Bertalanffy, Ludwig von, *General System Theory* (New York, 1968)
Bourbaki, Nicolas, 'L'Architecture des mathématiques' in *Les Grands Courants de la pensée mathématique*, ed. F. Le Lionnais (Paris, 1948)
Carroll, Lewis, 'What the Tortoise said to Achilles', in *Mind*, IV (1895), pp. 278–80.
Derrida, Jacques, 'La Mythologie Blanche (la métaphore dans le texte philosophique)' in *Poétique*, Seuil, Paris, no. 5 (1971): translated by F. C. T. Moore in *New Literary History*, vol. VI, Winter 1975, no. 2
Descartes, René, *Discours de la Méthode*
Dummett, Michael, *Frege: Philosophy of Language* (London, 1973)
Evans-Pritchard, E. E., *Witchcraft, Oracles and Magic among the Azande* (Oxford, 1937)
Foucault, Michel, *Les Mots et les choses* (Paris, 1966)
Frankfurt, Harry G., 'Freedom of the Will and the concept of a person', in *The Journal of Philosophy*, vol. LXVIII (1971)
Frege, Gottlob, *Translations from the Philosophical Writings of Gottlob Frege*, ed. P. Geach and M. Black (Oxford/New York, 1960)
Grice, Russell, *The Grounds of Moral Judgement* (Cambridge, 1967)
Hare, R. M., *The Language of Morals* (Oxford, 1961)
Hart, H. L. A., *The Concept of Law* (Oxford, 1961)
Kant, Immanuel, *Groundwork of the Metaphysic of Morals*, tr. H. J. Paton as *The Moral Law* (London, 1948)
Kenny, Anthony, *Action, Emotion and Will* (London, 1963)
Kovesi, Julius, *Moral Notions* (London, 1967)
Kreisel, G., 'Category Theory and the foundations of mathematics' in *Lecture Notes in Mathematics*, no. 106, Springer-Verlag, 1969, *Reports of the Mid-West Category Seminar: III*, pp. 233–47
Lévi-Strauss, Claude, *Mythologiques*, 4 vols. (Paris, 1964–71)
MacIntyre, Alasdair, *A Short History of Ethics* (London, 1966)
MacLane, Saunders, 'Foundations for Categories and Sets' in *Lecture Notes in Mathematics*, no. 92, Springer-Verlag, 1969, *Category Theory, Homology Theory and their Applications: II*, pp. 146–64

Mayo, Bernard, 'The Moral Agent', in *The Human Agent*, R. I. P. Lectures 1966–7 (London, 1968)

Mill, John Stuart, *On Liberty*

—— *Utilitarianism*

Monod, Jacques, *Le Hasard et la nécessité: essai sur la philosophie de la biologie moderne* (Paris, 1970); tr. A. Wainhouse as *Chance and Necessity* (New York, 1971/London, 1972)

Moore, F. C. T., *The Psychology of Maine de Biran* (Oxford, 1970)

Moore, G. E., *Principia Ethica* (Cambridge, 1903)

Piaget, Jean, *Le Structuralisme* (Paris, 1968); translated by C. Maschler (London, 1971)

Plato, *Phaedo*

Pörn, Ingmar, *The Logic of Power* (Oxford, 1970)

Propp, Vladimir, 'Transformations in Fairy Tales' in *Mythology: selected readings*, ed. P. Maranda (Harmondsworth, 1972)

Quine, W. V. O., 'Natural Kinds', in *Ontological Relativity and other Essays* (New York/London, 1969)

Rawls, John, *A Theory of Justice* (Oxford, 1972)

Ricœur, Paul, *Le Volontaire et l'involontaire* (Paris, 1963)

Saussure, Ferdinand de, *Course in General Linguistics*, ed. C. Bally & S. Sechehaye, tr. W. Baskin (New York, 1959)

Strawson, P. F., *Individuals* (London, 1959)

Teilhard de Chardin, Pierre, *Lettres à Leontine Zanta*, (Paris, 1965)

Thom, René, 'Structuralism and Biology', in *Towards a Theoretical Biology*, ed. C. H. Waddington (Edinburgh, 1972)

—— *Structural Stability and Morphogenesis*, tr. D. M. Fowler (Reading, Mass., 1975)

Warnock, G., *Contemporary Moral Philosophy* (London, 1967)

Wittgenstein, Ludwig, *Tractatus Logico-Philosophicus*, tr. D. F. Pears and B. F. McGuinness (London, 1961)

Index